HANDBOOK

OF THE

COLLECTION ILLUSTRATIVE OF THE WILD SILKS OF INDIA

HANDBOOK

OF THE

COLLECTION ILLUSTRATIVE OF THE WILD SILKS OF INDIA

THOMAS WARDLE

GYAN

Published by

Gyan Publishing House
5, Ansari Road
Daryaganj, New Delhi-110002
Phone: 011-47034999, 9811692060
E-mail: books@gyanbooks.com

Distribution Network
gyanbooks.com
India, USA, Canada, UK, Australia, France

ISBN : 978-81-212-9620-5 (PB)
First Published, 1881

2nd Impression 2023

Printed at: Gyan Press, Delhi.

HANDBOOK OF THE COLLECTION ILLUSTRATIVE OF THE WILD SILKS OF INDIA
Author: THOMAS WARDLE

THE WILD SILKS OF INDIA.

The Lords of the Committee of Council on Education think it desirable to direct public attention to the Collection illustrative of the Wild Silks of India which forms a part of the Indian Section added to the South Kensington Museum in December 1879*; and they have accordingly requested* MR. THOMAS WARDLE, *who has for several years paid special attention to the subject, to prepare this Handbook.*

They trust that this work may not only add largely to the interest of the Collection, but that it may lead to the further development of one of the most wide-spread and important natural productions of the Indian Empire, and thus be a means of increasing the material prosperity of Her Majesty's Indian subjects.

SOUTH KENSINGTON MUSEUM,
August 1881.

SCIENCE AND ART DEPARTMENT
OF THE COMMITTEE OF COUNCIL ON EDUCATION,
SOUTH KENSINGTON.

HANDBOOK

OF THE

COLLECTION ILLUSTRATIVE OF THE WILD SILKS OF INDIA,

IN THE

INDIAN SECTION OF THE SOUTH KENSINGTON MUSEUM,

WITH A

CATALOGUE OF THE COLLECTION AND NUMEROUS ILLUSTRATIONS.

BY THOMAS WARDLE.

1881.

CONTENTS.

ILLUSTRATIONS.

(The larvæ, cocoons, and moths are shown of the actual size.)

*** The illustrations have been engraved by Mr. Edmund Evans from drawings by Mr. W. H. Rider, Mr. G. R. Rigby and Mr. G. C. Wardle, students in the Leek Art Class, and Mr. F. Sugden. The drawings for Figs. 1, 2, 4, and 5, Plate I., Plates II. to VII., IX. to XXIX., and LV. were executed by Mr. W. H. Rider; for Plates XXX. to LIV. and LVI., by Mr. G. R. Rigby; for Fig. 3, Plate I., Plates LVII. to LXIII., and Figs. 1 and 2, Plate LXIV., by Mr. G. C. Wardle; for Fig. 3, Plate LXIV., Plates LXV. and LXVI., mechanical drawings, by Mr. F. Sugden.

I am glad to acknowledge the help I have received from my assistant Mr. J. T. Rigby in the microscopical examinations and other details.

T. W.

PREFACE.

Amongst the many names of persons in various countries interested in the cultivation of wild silkworms, the utilisation of their products, and the entomology of the subject, I venture to give the following list, which will be found interesting by many, and will serve to show to what a large extent this important subject has been made a matter of study and investigation. In England we have Dr. Roxburgh, Captain Hutton, Mr. Hugon, Dr. Birdwood, Mr. F. Moore, Mr. P. H. Gosse, Captain Mitchell, Mr. Butler, Major Coussmaker, Lady D. Neville, Lady Gilbert, Mr. Calvert, Mr. Geoghegan, Dr. Alex. Wallace, Dr. Mackenzie, Mr. E. Heycock, and others. On the Continent are M. Guérin Méneville, M. Personnat, M. Robert, M. Camille Mayne, M. W. Reed, M. Braine, M. Maurice Girard, M. Wailly, M. Costa, Wilhelm Carl Berg, M. Matthieu Bonagous, Mich. Judisky, Roo Van Westmas, N. H. de Graaf, Dr. Chavannes, and many others. My friend, M. Rondot, member of the Chamber of Commerce, Lyons, and President of the Silk Jury, class 34, at the Paris Exhibition of 1878, also author of several important works on silk and Eastern dyes, is at the present time giving much economic attention to this question, for the purpose of considering supply for the increasing demand of the French trade in wild silks.

Amongst those who have interested themselves especially in the utilisation of these wild silks must be mentioned Dr. Birdwood, C. S. I., who was one of the first, if not the first, to call public attention to the importance of Tusser silk, in a lengthy report to Government in 1858, which forms a useful and interesting appendix to this Handbook. (*See* Appendix I.)

Mr. Geoghegan is the author and compiler of a valuable report to the Government of India on the silk industy of India, dated 1874, and forming Part II. of "East India products" which is indispensable to a study of the subject.

Major Coussmaker is pursuing with a praiseworthy determination, at Poonah, the culture of Tusser silkworms, with a view of making Tusser silk as systematic an industry as that produced by *Bombyx mori* and the other mulberry silks.

Besides many others, the enthusiastic labours of the French, aided by their Société d'Acclimatation, set us a great example. They have succeeded in domesticating, if not in almost naturalising, several Eastern species of wild-silk producers, and in obtaining from them silk of some industrial value.

I would take this opportunity of mentioning that at the Paris Exhibition of 1878 the highest prize, a grand medal of honour, was awarded by the Jury of Class 34, Group 4, to the Indian Government on account of the collection of examples of the wild silks of India then exhibited. The medal was forwarded to His Excellency the Viceroy of India.

THOMAS WARDLE.

Leek, Staffordshire,
July 1881.

THE WILD SILKS OF INDIA.

CHAPTER I.

Classification of Wild Silkworms.

The term wild silks of India must be regarded as applying to all species of silk other than that produced by the *Bombyx mori*, the worm which feeds on the mulberry leaf, from which is obtained the silk of commerce by regular organised industries in Bengal, France, China, Japan, Italy, Persia, Siam, and in some other parts of the world.

For the most part, if not almost entirely, at present, the worms which produce these wild silks feed on the leaves of trees and plants which grow wild in the jungles and forests of India, or at any rate are not cultivated for silkworm food.

An impetus was given to the utilisation of these silks by the display of some of the most important of them at the Paris Exhibition in 1878, by Her Majesty's Government of India, in a collection which I had the honour of being appointed to arrange.

Since that time, as new uses have been found for Tusser silk, one of the chief and most widely spread of Indian wild silks, the question of supply has become a most important one.

The object of the present collection and of this Handbook is to draw public attention to the growing importance of the subject, and to present in as concise a form as its wide range will permit all information likely to be of either scientific or practical use.

It is believed the time is near when, by the aid of enterprise and capital, several species of the wild silks of India, not yet exported to England, will become as organised a production as the mulberry-fed silks, or the tea and cinchona planting of India; and this, not by simply collecting cocoons produced by the silkworms in their wild state, but by the systematic plantation of suitable food trees, careful attention to the rearing and breeding of the worms, the proper and timely collection of the cocoons, the application of proper reeling machinery, the collection of all the imperfect cocoons to be carded and spun by the elaborate machinery of Europe, and, lastly, by the adoption of my improvements and developments in dyeing and printing them, the results of a long and continuous course of study and experiment.

The value and importance of these silks have largely increased since it has been found that they now can, by suitable processes, be bleached, dyed, and printed into almost all shades of colour.

For several years I have been occupied in investigating the tinctorial adaptability of these silks, for the Government of India, under the direction of Sir Louis Mallet, C.B., Under Secretary of State for India, who has, with the Council, taken a warm interest in their gradual developments, the results of which are displayed in the present collection.

The silk-producing *Lepidopterous* insects are of many species, possessing very marked structural differences, whilst the variety and quiet beauty of their colours, and, with the exception of the mulberry feeders, their large size, contribute greatly to the charm of studying this branch of natural history, and they make a collection, apart from their great usefulness, worthy of being placed in the first rank.

They belong to the order *Lepidoptera*, and are all members of but two families, *Bombycidæ* and *Saturniidæ*.

All the *Saturniidæ* are silk spinners, but not all the *Bombycidæ*.

The British Museum Catalogue contains the names of 294 species of *Saturniidæ*. Mr. Butler, of the British Museum, informs me there have been 100 more species added since the publication of the catalogue.

The following table shows the position of these two families in the great system of classification of the animal kingdom :—

DIVISION III.—Articulata.

SUB-DIVISION II.—Anthropoda (or true articulata).

CLASS VIII.—Insecta.

SUB-CLASS III.—Metabola.

ORDER X.—Lepidoptera.

SUB-ORDER I.—Heterocera (Moths—8 groups or tribes).

GROUP.—Bombycina.

FAMILY 10.—*Genera.—Bombycidæ.*

Bombyx,	Ocinara,
Theophila,	Trilocha.

FAMILY 8.—*Genera.—Saturniidæ.*

Attacus,	Caligula,
Antheræa,	Neoris,
Actias,	Saturnia,
Salassa,	Loepa
Rinaca,	Cricula.
Rhodia,	

Mr. Frederic Moore has kindly furnished me with the following list of all the silk-producing *Lepidoptera* of India known at the present time. It is the most complete one yet published, and shows how rich India is in silk-producing insects:—

MULBERRY-FEEDING SILKWORMS—DOMESTICATED.

Bombyx mori (Linnæus).—The common silkworm, domesticated in China, Bokhara, Afghanistan, Cashmere, Persia, S. Russia, Turkey, Egypt, and Algeria, Italy, France, and Spain, in all which countries it produces but one crop annually, spinning the largest cocoon and the best silk, of a golden yellow, or white.

Bombyx textor (Hutton).—The *Boro poolloo* of Bengal, domesticated in S. China and Bengal; an annual only, producing a white (sometimes yellow) cocoon, of a different texture and more flossy than *B. mori.*

Bombyx sinensis (Hutton).—The *Sina, Cheena,* or small Chinese monthly worm of Bengal, partially domesticated in Bengal, where it was introduced from China; produces several broods in the year; cocoon white and yellow.

Bombyx cræsi (Hutton).—The *Nistry* or *Madrassee* of Bengal, introduced from China; domesticated in Bengal; yielding seven or eight broods of golden yellow cocoons in the year, of larger size than *B. sinensis.*

Bombyx fortunatus (Hutton).—The *Dasee* of Bengal yields several broods annually, spinning the smallest cocoon of a golden yellow colour.

Bombyx Arracanensis (Hutton).—The Burmese silkworm, domesticated in Arracan, said to have been introduced from China through Burmah; yields several broods annually; cocoons larger than the Bengal monthly species.

Mulberry-feeding Silkworms—Wild.

Theophila Huttoni (Westwood).—The wild silkworm of the N.W. Himalayas. A wild species, the worms being found abundantly feeding on the indigenous mulberry in the mountain forests of the N. W. Himalayas.

Theophila Sherwilli (Moore).—The wild silkworm of the S.E. Himalayas.

Theophila Bengalensis (Hutton).—The wild silkworm of Lower Bengal. Discovered in the neighbourhood of Calcutta feeding on *Artocarpus lacoocha*. Found also at Ranchee, in Chota Nagpore.

Theophila religiosa (Helfer).—The *Joree* of Assam and *Deo-mooga* of Cachar. Feeds on the bur tree (*Ficus indica*) and the pipul (*F. religiosæ*).

Theophila mandarina (Moore).—The wild silkworm of Chekiang, N. China. Worms stated to feed on wild mulberry trees, spinning a white cocoon.

Ocinara lactea (Hutton).—Mussooree, N. W. Himalaya. Feeds on *Ficus venosa*, spinning a small yellow cocoon, yielding several broods during the summer.

Ocinara Moorei (Hutton).—Mussooree, N.W. Himalaya. Also feeds on *Ficus venosa*, as well as on the wild fig, spinning a small white cocoon. It is a multivoltine.

Ocinara diaphana (Moore).—Khasia hills.

Trilocha varians (Walker).—N. and S. India.

Atlas and Eria Group.

Attacus atlas (Linnæus).—China, Burmah, India, Ceylon, Java. This appears to be almost omnivorous, feeding in different districts upon the shrubs and trees peculiar to them. At Mussooree it is found upon *Bradleia ovata*, *Falconeria insignis*, and several other trees; at Almorah the yellow-flowering barberry is said to be its favourite food. In Cachar it feeds on various other trees. Cocoon well stored with a fine silk.

Attacus silhetica (Helfer).—Silhet.

Attacus Edwardsia (White).—Sikkim, Cherra, and Khasia hills.

Attacus cynthia (Drury).—China. Domesticated in the provinces of Shantung and Honan. Feeds on the varnish tree (*Ailanthus glandulosa*).

Attacus ricini (Jones).—The *Eria* of Assam, and *Arindi* of Dinajpore. Domesticated in the Northern parts of Bengal (Bogra, Rungpore, and Dinajpore), in Assam and

Cachar, feeding on the castor-oil plant (*Ricinus communis*), yielding seven or more crops annually. Cocoons somewhat loose and flossy, orange red, sometimes white. The so-called "Ailanthus silkworm" of Europe—the result of a fertile hybrid between the Chinese and the Bengal species, was produced some years ago in France, by Monsieur Guérin-Méneville, and subsequently reared, from whence it was introduced into various parts of the world.

Attacus Cunningi (Hutton).—N.W. Himalayas. Common in a wild state, feeding on the leaves of *Coriaria nipalensis* and *Xanthophyllum hostile*. Cocoons hard and compactly woven, rusty orange or grey. An annual.

Attacus lunula (Walker).—Silhet.

Attacus obscurus (Butler).—Cachar. Not very common. Stated to feed on a plant called *Lood*.

Attacus Guérini (Moore).—Eastern Bengal.

Actias Group.

Actias Selene (McLeay).—Mussooree, Sikkim, and Khasia hills; Madras. The worms feed upon *Andromeda ovalifolia*, *Coriaria nipalensis*, wild cherry, and walnut, at Mussooree, and on *Odina wodier* in Madras.

Actias Sinensis (Walker).—N. China.

Actias Leto (Doubleday).—Sikkim and Khasia hills.

Actias Mœnas (Doubleday).—Sikkim and Khasia hills.

Actias ignescens (Moore).—Andaman Isles.

Tusser and Moonga Group.

Antheræa mylitta (Drury).—*Antheræa paphia* of authors; the *Tasar*, *Tusser*, *Tussar*, or *Tussah* silkworm.

These well-known and valuable insects (of various undetermined species) are widely distributed over India, from east to west and north to south, on the coast, and in the Central Provinces. They feed in a wild state upon the ber (*Zizyphus jujuba*), the asun (*Terminalia alata*), the seemul (*Bombax heptaphyllum*), &c.

Antheræa mezankooria (Moore); the *Mezankoorie* silkworm of the Assamese.—The worms which produce the mezankoorie silk are stated to feed on the addakoory (? *Tetranthera sp.*), which is abundant in Upper and Lower Assam. The silk is nearly white, its value being 50 per cent. above that of the moonga.

Antheræa nebulosa (Hutton).—This is the *Tusser* of the Sonthal jungles of Colong. It is also found in Singbhoom, Chota Nagpore

Antheræa Perrotteti (Guér. Mén.).—Described as being found in the districts of Pondicherry, feeding upon a species of *Zizyphus*, the jambool (*Syzygium jambolanum*), &c. Stated to produce four broods in a year.

Antheræa Andamana (Moore).—An allied species to the Tusser. Inhabits the S. Andamans.

Antheræa Frithii (Moore).—Sikkim Himalayas. A common species, inhabiting the hot sub-tropical valleys below 2,000 ft. Known only as a wild species. The cocoon is stated to be similar to that of the Tusser in form, but of finer silk.

Antheræa Helferi (Moore).—Sikkim Himalayas. This is a common species found in the hot valleys of Sikkim.

Antheræa Assama (Helfer).—The *Moonga* or *Mooga* of the Assamese. The moonga silkworm feeds upon the trees known in Assam as the champa (*Michelia sp.*), the soom, kontoolva, digluttee (*Tetranthera diglottica*), the pattee shoonda (*Laurus obtusifolia*), and the Sonhalloo (*Tet. macrophylla*). It is extensively cultivated by the natives, and can be reared in houses, but is fed and thrives best in the open air and upon the trees. The silk forms an article of export from Assam, and leaves the country generally in the shape of thread.

Antheræa Roylei (Moore).—The oak-feeding silkworm of the N.W. Himalayas. A common species, feeding on the hill oak (*Quercus incana*) of the N.W. Himalayas (Simla, Masuri, Almora). The cocoon is large and very tough, the silk being pronounced promising, and worth cultivating. They can be reared easily in the house.

Miscellaneous Group.

Salassa Lola (Westwood).—Sikkim Himalayas.

Rinaca Zuleika (Hope).—Sikkim.

Rhodia Newara (Moore).—Nepal (Kathmandoo). Worms feed upon a species of weeping willow. Spins a brilliant green cocoon, pendent from the twigs.

Caligula Thibeta (Westwood).—Mussooree, N.W. Himalayas, 7,000 ft. Common, the worms feeding on *Andromeda ovalifolia*, wild pear, and the cultivated quince, forming a light, open, net-like cocoon.

Caligula Simla (Westwood).—Simla, N.W. Himalayas, 5,000 ft. Feeds on the walnut, *Salix Babylonica*, wild pear, &c.; forms an open, net-like cocoon.

Caligula Cachara (Moore.)—Cachar.

Neoris Huttoni (Moore).—Mussooree, N.W. Himalaya,

6,500 feet. The worms appear in April, feeding upon a species of wild-pear tree; spins a thin silken cocoon.

Neoris Shadulla (Moore).—Yarkund.

Neoris Stoliczkana (Felder).—Ladak.

Saturnia Cidosa (Moore). Hot valleys of the Sikkim Himalayas.

Saturnia Grotei (Moore).—Sikkim Himalayas.

Saturnia Lindia (Moore).—Sikkim Himalayas.

Saturnia Anna (Moore).—Sikkim Himalayas.

Loepa katinka (Westwood).—Sikkim, 5,000 to 7,000 feet. Assam.

Loepa Sikkima (Moore).—Hot valleys of Sikkim.

Loepa sivalica (Hutton.)—Mussooree, 5,000 feet. Spins a long cocoon, pointed at each end, and of a dark greenish-grey colour.

Loepa miranda (Moore).—Sikkim Himalayas.

Cricula trifenestrata (Helfer); the *Haumpottonee* of the Assamese.—Noted as being very common in Assam, the worms feeding on the soon tree, forming an open net-like cocoon of a beautiful yellow colour and of a rich lustre, the silk being spun in the same manner as the Eria cocoon. Occurs also in Moulmein, where the worms are stated to feed upon the cashew-nut tree (*Anacardium orientale*).

Cricula drepanoides (Moore).—Sikkim.

To this number may be added a few others which, although not of India, are well worth the attention of the Government of India for the purpose of acclimatisation there.

Antheræa Pernyi (Guér. Mén.)—The oak-feeding silk-worm of Mantchouria, N. China. This is described as having been long known to the Mantchour Tartars, very large quantities of the silk used among the Chinese. The worms feed on various species of oak (*Quercus Mongalica*, &c.), the cocoon differing from the Tusser in form and texture. The silk is represented as strong, but with little lustre. Two crops of silk are produced in the year—a spring and autumn crop.

Antheræa Confuci (Moore).—A species allied to *A. pernyi*, inhabiting the hills in the neighbourhood of Shanghai, N. China.

Antheræa Yama-mai (Guérin Méneville).—The *Yama-mai* silkworm of Japan.

An oak-feeding species, forming a cocoon of a pale yellowish-green colour. This worm feeds on the oak, and produces excellent silk of considerable commercial value in Japan. I should strongly recommend its introduction into

India. It has been acclimatised in Europe, and, crossed with *Bombyx attacus Pernyi*, is successfully reared in France, the eggs hatching at almost freezing point. The silk is much cultivated and used in Japan. Its fibre is oval, and 950th of an inch thick.

Saturnia pyretorum, from South China.—The worm feeds upon the *Liquidamber formosana* in Canton, Amoy, where the silk is stated to be woven into a coarse fabric.

Neoris shadulla (Moore).—Yarkund.

Theophila mandarina (Moore).—N. China.

CHAPTER II.

History of Silk.

It may be useful to give a brief history of the silk of commerce in introducing to the reader the wild silks of India.

The Chinese appear to be the first people who applied themselves to sericulture.

The words "Seres," used by Theophanes, and "Serinda," by Procopius, were in all probability so used to indicate that part of the East, which was no doubt China, where the silk industry existed at a very remote period.

Dr. Birdwood states* that Ptolemy was the first to use the word *Serice* for China, or rather, the northern part of it, known later as Cathay; and that the word is derived from the Chinese name of the silkworm, *see*, in Corean *sir*, whence the Greek Σήρ, the silkworm; Σῆρες, the people furnishing silk; and Σηρικόν, *serikon*, silk. The Latin *sericum* had been traced direct to the Mongol *sirkeh;* and the *serikoth* of Isaiah, xix. 9, has been supposed to be silk. Of the same root as the Latin *sericum* is the French *soie*, the German *seiden*, the Russian *sheolk*, the Anglo-Saxon *seolc*, the Icelandic *silke*, and the English *silk*. In Persian, silk is *ab-resham;* in Hindustani *reshm;* in Arabic *khuz;* in Malay *sutra;* in Tamil *pattu*.

We are informed by Hawae-nan-tze, in a Chinese work called the "Silkworm Classic," that Te-ling-she, the principal queen of Hwang-te, B.C. 2640, was the first to

---

* See "Discussion" printed with the Author's lecture on the Wild Silks of India before the Society of Arts, London, May 9, 1879.

rear silkworms, and the Emperor Hwang-te was induced to invent robes and garments from this circumstance.

But Dr. Balfour states* as follows : "There seems to be no doubt that China is the country where the product of the silkworm was first used as a material for textile fabrics, and that the industry has gradually radiated from China, as a centre, till it covers, at the present day, a number of very widely distributed areas of very diverse climatic conditions. The Chinese historians carry back the cultivation of the mulberry and the breeding of silkworms to the period of myths. If they are to be believed, the art of silk reeling was known in China in the time of Fouh-hi, a century before the date usually assigned to the Biblical deluge, and the Empress Si-ling-chi, wife of the celebrated Hoang-ti (2,602 years before the Chistian era) did not disdain to share in the labours attending the care of the insect, as well as in those of the loom, the invention of which seems to be attributed to her, and to have raised her to the position of a tutelary genius, with special altars of her own. But whatever the precise date of the discovery, it appears there can be no question of the very high antiquity of the knowledge of the worm and its product in China. A series of imperial edicts and a voluminous literature of practical treatises testify to the importance of the industry and the care that was taken to foster an art which was considered, according to M. de Rosny, 'best fitted to promote the morality of the people and extinguish pauperism in the empire.'"

The queen and wives of the nobles through successive generations personally attended to the rearing of the silkworms.

That this silk was of the mulberry-fed kind is evident from a further extract from the "Silkworm Classic," which says that afterwards, "when Yu regulated the waters, B.C. " 2200, mention is made in his work on the tribute of the " land adapted for the mulberry tree having been supplied " with silkworms, from which time the advantage thereof " gradually increased."†

It is not known whether silk was utilised in India at so early a period as this, probably not ; but that India learned the art from China is generally understood, although at what period is not known.

About the middle of the sixth century, the Western World received a supply of silkworms' eggs. These were conveyed

---

* Cyclopædia of India, vol. 5, p. 335.

† Horsfield and Moore's Catalogue, p. 377.

from China to Constantinople by two Persian monks, who had gone to the East as missionaries, and had observed in China the various processes connected with the rearing of silkworms, the nature of the trees on which they fed, and the preparation of the silk. This occurred in the year 552, in the reign of Justinian, who gave every encouragement to the introduction of the valuable insect. The eggs were secrectly conveyed from China within a hollow cane; at the proper season they were hatched, and the caterpillars were fed on the leaves of the wild mulberry tree. The monks continued to superintend at Constantinople the rearing of the insects and the whole process of manufacturing the silk. From this small commencement the myriads of silkworms have sprung which throughout Eastern and Western Asia have met the demand for silk, which has gone on increasing from that time to the present.

For more precise information respecting the westward spread of silk culture, I would strongly recommend to my readers Dr. Birdwood's excellent Handbook to the British India Section of the Paris Exhibition, p. 104; and to his later volume, "Indian Art," published as a Handbook to the new India Section of the South Kensington Museum. These learned histories of silk will be read with much pleasure by all who can see in silken stuffs something more than a mere commercial value. The account of its utilisation and spread from East to West is described with almost the charm of romance. Its development is traced from its earliest days in the East to its introduction at last into our own country in the reign of Henry VI., and again to the times of the persecution of the Huguenots by Louis XIV., which drove their silk workers by a happy tide to our shores. How that tide has in our own times returned to France, and carried with it, not the workers, but the industry, I leave for statesmen and manufacturers to think over and retrieve.

Europe may almost be said to have got hold of the silk industry by a fraud; the two monks before mentioned brought away the eggs from China concealed in their walking canes. A similar account is well related by Dr. A. Wallace of the way the eggs of the prized *Yama-mai* silkworm were abstracted from Japan by a young Japanese, who, at the instigation of his European tutor, obtained them at the risk of his life, for this was an offence there punishable by death. A further account of the circumstances connected with this event will be found at page 65. It would be but a small return for the benefits we have obtained to ourselves by these frauds if we could teach those weaker peoples the benefits of the better making, and above all the more friendly interchanging, of stuffs and commodities. It is with this hope that I have arranged the present collection; that, having India, with its extensive wild-silk regions, in our possession, we may, by gentle means, teach the native to improve the culture and preliminary stages of its manufacture, so that it may be brought from them in a state fit to be used by us for all the purposes of which it is really capable; and, to use the words of Sir Louis Mallet in the first letter of instruction I received from the India Office, that "a new and very profitable industry may be founded in India."

The natural history of every kind of silk may be briefly stated to be this: From a small egg laid by the moth, of whatever species, appears in due season a small larva, or caterpillar, or worm, as it is usually called. This worm, after having lived its day, feeding only on the leaves of certain plants characteristic of its species, and increasing in size, spins, or rather secretes, a fine silk thread around itself for covering and protection during the time it lies dormant in the next stage of its existence. As soon as it has secreted all the silk, it changes into a pupa or chrysalis, and remains inside its silken cell until the time for its appearance as an *imago* or perfect moth, having four scaly wings, with six legs and two antennæ, which are larger in the male than in the female. When its hybernation is ended it emits a fluid which softens the end of its cocoon cell, and, by means of its wing spines and legs, parts the fibres aside until the opening is large enough for it to creep out. After a short time its wings expand and dry, and it enters into its perfect state.

It lives only a few days in this phase of its existence. It is in this stage only that the race is perpetuated, the female laying a number of eggs, and dying soon afterward.

CHAPTER III.

The Silk of Commerce.

The silk which is generally known as the silk of commerce, in both ancient and modern days, is distinguished from all others by the singular circumstance of the larvæ (Plate I., Fig. 3) which produce it being fed only on the leaves of the mulberry tree (Plate XL.) The moth (Plate I., Figs. 1 and 2) is therefore named *Bombyx mori.*

It must not be inferred, however, that there is only one species, as is too generally thought. Mr. F. Moore assures me there is sufficient structural variation in moths which were at one time understood to be *Bombyx mori* to constitute a specific difference. The following species feed on the mulberry, and their silk is in ordinary and promiscuous use along with that of the *mori* :—

Bombyx sinensis (Hutton),
Bombyx crœsi (Hutton),
Bombyx fortunatus (Hutton),
Bombyx arracanensis (Hutton),
Bombyx textor (Hutton),

and no doubt several others not yet defined, but whose silk varies vary much, such as that called *Canton* and that called *Tsatlee*, although both are from China, as well as the silk from Japan, which has a thicker fibre than the *mori* silk of other countries, being $\frac{1}{1650}$ of an inch thick, as against $\frac{1}{2100}$ of an inch of the *mori* silk of Italy. The strength and tension of this and the wild silks, as well as the respective sizes of their cocoons, are given in my table of microscopic measurements on page 68, which I have carefully revised. I commend the study of this table to all engaged in silk manufacturing, whether of ordinary or wild silks, as I consider the results of the highest importance. In the column of relative strengths it will be seen that the breaking strength of a single fibre of *Bombyx mori* or mulberry-fed silk is $2\frac{3}{8}$ drams, whilst the weight of 7 drams is required to break a single fibre of *Tusser* silk.

The eggs of *Bombyx mori* and the other species of *Bombyx* form a most important article of commerce between Japan and Europe. They are imported from Japan into Italy and the South of France annually, to supply the deficiency caused by the silkworm disease known as pebrine, and also to infuse, as it were, new blood. The value of the eggs is about 25*s*. per oz.. Twelve pounds of cocoons are required to produce one pound of silk. The value of the raw silk of Bengal in London is now from 14*s*. to 18*s*. per lb. The colour is generally of a rich golden yellow; but it is also sometimes white. In China and Japan it is all white, with rare exceptions.

CHAPTER IV.

WILD SILKS.

As far as I can learn, the only species of silk at present utilised in India besides those of the several species of mulberry-feeding worms of the genus *Bombyx* are the wild ones of the following species:—

Antheræa mylitta, or Tusser worm.
„ *Assama*, or Muga worm.
„ *perotteti.*
„ *nebulosa.*
„ *Roylei.*
„ *Frithii.*
„ *mezankooria.*
Attacus ricini, or Eria worm.
„ *atlas*, or Atlas worm.
„ *Edwardsia.*
Cricula trifenestrata.
And perhaps
Attacus selene and *Antheræa Helferi.*

Of these only *Antheræa mylitta*, *A. Assama*, and *Attacus ricini* have been utilised to any important extent, although, in addition to them, there is in India a large number of other species which produce silk cocoons.

The Indian localities of the four principal ones, *Ricini*, *Atlas*, *Muga*, and *Tusser*, are shown on the maps, Plates XXIV., XXV., XXVI., XXVII., by shading.

The unshaded spaces, representing large portions of territory, on each map, are not left unshaded because the districts they represent do not produce the respective silks, but because I have received no reports from the India Office which give any account of their being found there. I believe the Tusser worm will be found to be productive over the whole of India and also of British Burma.

The only wild silk at present exported from India is the *Tusser*, which I shall describe in the following chapter.

CHAPTER V.

TUSSER SILKWORM AND SILK.

The most important Indian wild silk is that known as *Tusser*, *Tussah*, or perhaps more properly spelled *Tasar*.

As there are several modes of spelling this word, I add a table of synonyms showing them :—

Tasar.—Name in India for both the *Tusser* worm and the silk.

Tussore.—French.

Bombyx scide.—German.

Tusser, Tussah, Tussa, Tussar, Tusseh, modes of spelling used in England, no doubt derived from the Hindostani word *Tusuru,* which means a shuttle.

Tusser silk is the product of the larva of the moth *Antheræa mylitta* of Linnæus (Plate II., Figs. 1 and 2).

This species is also known by the following synonyms :—

Phalæna Attacus mylitta (Drury).
Bombyx mylitta (Fabricius).
Antheræa mylitta (Hübner).
Attacus mylitta (Blanchard).
Saturnia mylitta (Westwood).
Phalæna paphia (Roxburgh).*
Saturnia paphia (Helfer).
Bughy silkworm moth of the Beerbhoom Hills.
Kolissurra silkworm moth of the Mahrattas.

There is but little doubt that this silk has been utilised for many centuries both in India and China, but I have not been able to find any important account of its ancient history.

One of the earliest notices of this insect, or of a species very nearly related to it, is given by the venerable Rumphius, who was born at Hanau in 1657, in his "Herbarium Amboinense" (dedicated by him to the East India Company), vol. iii. p. 113, pl. 75; he discovered the larvæ in Amboina feeding on the *Mangium caseolari rubrum* (*Rhizophora caseolaris,* Linn.), a plant of the order of *Terebintaceæ.*† He says :—

"When I had kept the cocoons for three weeks a moth came out quite perfect, which was the most beautiful and largest I had ever seen, which, biting away the silk, showed its head, and at the same time drew out with it a little flock of yellow silk; this the moth performed at night. Its body, like all other moths', is a dirty yellow colour, and in length two joints of a finger; it has two downy horns on its head of a golden hue, and four large wings, of which the two largest are about an inch long and of a golden

* Not of Linnæus. The true *P. Paphia* is an African species (*F. Moore*).
† Horsfield and Moore's catalogue of Lepidopterous insects, pp. 386, 387.

colour, but a purple line runs through them transversely and every wing has, as it were, in its middle a window-like eye, which is surrounded by a purple circle, and, as it were, of the transparency of glass."

The larvæ, when fully grown, are about four inches in length; they have twelve joints or articulations, besides their extremities; their colour is green, resembling the leaves on which they feed; and they are marked with reddish spots and a reddish-yellow band running length-ways. They feed on the following plants:—

Rhizophora calceolaris (Linn.).
Terminalia alata glabra (Assum tree).
Terminalia tomentosa (the saj tree).
Terminalia catappa (country almond tree).
Tectona grandis (teak tree).
Zizyphus jujuba (ber tree).
Shorea robusta (sal tree).
Bombax heptaphyllum (Semul).
Careya sphærica.
Pentaptera tomentosa.
Pentaptera glabra.
Ricinus communis (castor-oil plant).
Cassia lanceolata.
Lagerstræmia Indica, vern. Daiyeti.
Carissa Carandas, ,, Karinda.
Terminalia arjuna ,, Sádara.
Ficus Benjaminia ,, Nándruk.

Major Coussmaker remarks:—

"The *Daiyeti* (*Lagerstræmia Indica*) is a most promising plant for feeding the *Tusser* worm, as the harder it is cut back and eaten off by the worms the more luxuriantly it throws up shoots, especially when watered liberally; these shoots are clothed with leaves the whole way up, and the caterpillars greedily devour every bit of leaf, and even the more succulent parts of the shoots. I have not been able to raise this plant from seed, but find that the roots have excessive vitality.

"The *Bher* (*Zizyphus jujuba*) is the tree on which, in the Deccan, the greatest number of cocoons are found. It grows very thickly, but only from seed, as far as my experience goes. The leaves are rather sparsely distributed, and the growth is very straggling. The caterpillars eat up every leaf, and also devour the flowers. The *Karinda* (*Carissa Carandas*) is more leafy than the Bher, and the caterpillars also eat it off very closely, but it recovers leaves slowly, and the plant does not grow quickly. The *Ani* (*Terminalia tomentosa*) and the *Sádára* (*Terminalia arjuna*) have much larger leaves than the preceding shrubs, but they grow very slowly, at all events for the first two years of their existence; the *Ani* is the favourite food of the worm in the Konkan. The *Nandruk* plants planted by me have not thriven well, nor did the worms feed on them this last monsoon, though on the more elevated country from Satara towards the south I have found many cocoons on this tree."

Mr. Watkins, of Messrs. Watkins and Doncaster, naturalists of London, has succeeded in raising *Tusser* worms, I believe, for the first time in England, and has some now feeding on oak leaves; the evergreen oak appears to be the best.

In six weeks from the time they are hatched the worms begin to spin their cocoons, which they most curiously suspend from the branches of the trees by constructing a thick hard cord or pedicle of silky matter, exuded before spinning commences, which is made to grasp the branches. (Plate IV., Fig. 1).

Major Coussmaker remarks that in 1878, in his establishment, the first worm was hatched on the 15th June and the last spun its cocoon on the 15th November.

Tusser silk is found, as will be seen by referring to the map, Plate XXIV., over nearly the whole of India.

In the Central Provinces, Mr. Geoghegan says, Tusser is utilised in Raipore, Bilaspore, Tumbulpore, the Upper Godavery, Chanda, Bhundora, Nagpore, Balaghat, Seonee, Chindwara, Beetool, and Nursinghpore. Sumbulpore is said to yield 3,500 seers (7,000 lbs.) of silk; Raipore, 6,000 (12,000 lbs.); Bilaspore, 900 (1,800 lbs.); and Chanda, 22,500 (45,000 lbs.). The silk is woven and used in the Provinces in mixed fabrics of cotton warp and Tusser weft. But, at any rate in some districts, muktahs (garments worn by Brahmins after bathing), cholees (women's bodices), and deputtas and dorwas seem to be made of pure Tusser silk.

Captain Brooke* says:—

"In Seonee it is a regular organised and thoroughly understood industry, from the rearing of the insects to the weaving of silk into cloth, with all its accompanying machinery of trade guilds, money lenders, &c. This state of things is, in my opinion, no disadvantage; for, in place

---

* Geoghegan, "Silk Industry of India, p. 199."

of having to contend with the difficulties which in India always surround the introduction of anything new or unknown, the demand is all that is necessary to stimulate production to any extent required. Nor is this a figure of speech, for the natural food of the *Tussar* worm is the leaves of the *saj*, *lendeya*, and *dhowra* trees, all of which are found in every part of this district, and are, I believe, common to the whole of Gondwana. These trees are, besides, propagated with facility, and, as far as the requirement of the insect goes, are of rapid growth; hence, if the silk became more known and better valued, and the profits sufficiently attractive, we might witness a development of the culture similar in kind to that which has of late years taken place in the case of cotton. Supposing, then, a demand to spring up, I am of opinion that the supply would, in a very short time, amply meet it. The nucleus of no inconsiderable trade now exists, and only awaits the stimulus of high prices.

"The primary question whether the product is, or may become, of such value as to occasion a large demand, is one, perhaps, that more nearly concerns traders than Indian administrators; still, so convinced am I of the value and beauty of the fabric that can be woven from well-reeled *Tasar* that I would venture to strongly urge Government action in introducing it to the markets of Europe."

The worms require protection from birds and ants, which are their greatest enemies. The first cocoons are made in August, and are sold, after the moth has escaped, to the silk dealers at 4 to 8 pice (1½*d.* to 3*d.*) the hundred. The unpierced cocoons are only sold to rearers, as seed, at 1.8 rupees to 2 rupees (3*s.* to 4*s.*) per hundred.

Captain Brooke says:—

"In Chanda and Bilaspoor, Central Provinces, the rearing of the worms is attended by many ceremonial observances, which begin when the insect leaves the egg, and are not discontinued until the cocoons are gathered and taken to the rearer's house. During the feeding of the worm the Dheemurs lead lives of the strictest abstinence.

"No female is allowed within a considerable distance of the trees upon which the worms are feeding, and if by chance a woman or impure man passes near the feeding grounds the trees and worms are sprinkled in the name of Jogní (an incarnation of the god Mahadeo, whom the worms are supposed to represent) with water taken, if procurable, from a running stream, and in which *tulsí* leaves have been steeped. During the same period the

Dheemurs carefully abstain from flesh, fish, or haldí as their food, nor do they cut their hair or shave, and carefully deny themselves all ablution. When the cocoons are formed they are collected into a heap, and a goat, pig, or fowl is sacrificed to Mahadeo in his form Jogní; the blood is sprinkled over the cocoons, and, after a bout of liquor, are taken home. On the third day following the Dheemurs shave and resume their normal condition.*"

The caterpillars moult five times, at intervals of from five to eight days. When first hatched they weigh but $\frac{1}{5}$ of a grain, and are about $\frac{1}{4}$ of an inch long; but at the end of their larval existence, which is from forty to forty-five days, they have attained a size of seven inches long, one inch in diameter, and weigh about 370 grains (Plate III.) They then begin to spin their cocoons, which are of an egg shape and silvery drab in colour (Plate IV., Fig. 1). The silk is all regularly deposited in a compact manner, resembling in substance the shell of an egg (Plate IV., Fig. 2).

The cocoons vary much in size. The largest I have seen are from Sambulpoor, and are two inches long and $1\frac{1}{4}$ inches in diameter. The weight of the large cocoons is, without the pupa and supporting pedicle, 28 grains; the ordinary size 16 grains. Mr. H. Meyer, of Milan, has reeled for me an unbroken double thread from one cocoon, which weighs 12 grains, and measures 1,332 yards, or a little more than three quarters of a mile.

Major Coussmaker remarks †:—

"As a rule, there are certainly two crops in the year; the moths of the first batch come out in about four or six weeks after the first lot of worms (which come out at the commencement of the rains) have spun; those of the second batch remain quiescent until the rains begin again, that is to say, until May. As this entails the chrysalis remaining in the cocoon as long as eight months, exposed to the hottest sun and occasional thunderstorms, the cocoon had need to be made a hard impenetrable material; so indestructible is it, that Bheels and and other tribes which live in the jungles use the cocoon as an extinguisher to the bamboo tube in which they keep the "falita" or cotton-rope tinder used by them for lighting their tobacco and the slow matches of their matchlocks. The cocoon is also cut into a long spiral band, and used for binding the barrel of matchlocks to the stocks, being, as the natives say, un-

* Captain Brooke, as quoted in Geoghegan, "Silk Industry of India," p. 110.
† "The Tusser Silkworm," p. 9, 1873.

affected either by water or fire. The cocoon consists of two kinds of silk; what it first spins is reddish, and of this the pedicle and outside network are made. This silk consists of threads of different lengths, but the rest is generally unbroken from beginning to end of the cocoon.

"After the caterpillar has spun a layer of silk thick enough to conceal itself, it discharges some kind of gum or cement, thick like plaster of paris, and with its muscular action it causes this secretion to thoroughly permeate the whole cocoon and solidify the wall. In this manner it goes on spinning layer after layer of loops, and cementing them altogether until the whole of its silk is exhausted, and the wall of the cocoon becomes so hard that it requires a sharp penknife to cut through it. The ring at the end of the pedicle, which has been spun round the twig, is a most necessary provision of nature; for it often happens that either the caterpillar has been unable to attach its cocoon to a leaf, or that during the long time the cocoon remains unburst on the tree the leaf or leaves to which the cocoon was at first attached become separated from it, and the cocoon hangs suspended to the twig like a berry."

After eight or nine months in the pupa state a moist spot is observed at one end of the cocoon. The moth is now about to emerge both from its pupa shell and from the cocoon. It secretes an acid fluid which softens the cement of the cocoon, and enables it to separate the fibres sufficiently to allow of its creeping out, it being no doubt assisted in this by its short pointed spines. The head of the moth first appears with its antennæ, broad in the male and narrow in the female, thus enabling the observer to note the sex and to put them in pairs. The male moth generally flies away the night of his exit from the cocoon, after his wings become extended and dried.

The female rarely flies off, but during the first three days of her existence she lays her eggs, which hatch about 12 days afterwards. The new life of the moth does not extend to more than eleven days. As will be seen from Plate II., the moth is a fine and handsome insect. It measures across the wings about six inches in the male and about five inches in the female. Notice the vitreous and transparent wing spots. They are like those of the Atlas moth, but smaller; they are regarded with superstitious reverence by the natives, who see in them a resemblance to the chakra or discus of the god Vishnu, and from this consider the moth a sacred insect.* The colour of the moth

* Geoghegan.

is reddish-brown in the male, but the female is much yellower.

Major Coussmaker has formed a breeding establishment at Poonah, and has planted many young trees for feeding the worm. He has changed his former plan of feeding them on cut twigs brought to them in captivity, and now allows them, carefully watched, to feed in the open air on the growing shrubs. This was an evident change for the better. The larvæ moulted in four to five days, instead of five to eight days; they spun their cocoons in 28 to 35 days, instead of from 40 to 50 days, and the moths emerged from the cocoons in 30 days, their eggs proving more fertile than under the former plan.

A report on Tusser culture from Major Coussmaker is dated Poonah, February 21st, 1880, from which I have extracted a few particulars:—

"The great difficulty in rearing the *Tusser* worm is to ensure an unfailing supply of suitable food, and, in order to obtain this, the shrubs should be planted in the form of hedges. I am in favour of growing Daiyeti (*Lagerstrœmia Indica*), an ornamental shrub fairly abundant in the cantonment of Poonah, thickly planted on ridges so as to form continuous lines of food, while the Bher (*Zizyphus jujuba*) and the Kārinda (*Carissa Carandas*) might be planted as hedges surrounding the plantation, as they naturally grow into thick tangled masses, and, being thorny, would keep out cattle. In three years the Bher will grow from seed into a bush four feet high, and in the same time the Daiyeti raised from cuttings and root suckers would be nearly as high, and the whole plantation would be ready for feeding by the commencement of the third monsoon after it had been started. I should, if possible, lay it out with a view of irrigating it, for, though there is no necessity to water the trees during the rainy season, still liberal watering and plenty of manure will always increase the supply of leaf; by high cultivation of this nature my small plantation is now so far advanced that next monsoon I hope to be able to state how much ground will be required for a definite number of worms.

"Last year the worms finished spinning their cocoons in the early part of November, and it appeared to me that when the cold east winds which we had at the end of October set in the worms made no further progress, and more of them died at that time, instead of spinning their cocoons, than at any other period of their existence. During the five months I was rearing them this last season

I could not detect any epidemic or any well-defined sickness among them, nor did there appear any difference in those reared in the open or in the shade, or on the large or small trees, or under cover; insects, birds, mice, rats, squirrels, and lizards carried them off repeatedly, but the reason of so much life being lost was that I tried to preserve more than I had food for; in fact, they died from preventible accidents.

"One of the most interesting, and I think important, facts that I have this year been able to prove, is with regard to the composition of the cement with which the caterpillar hardens its cocoon.

"Former analyses of this agent made for me, in England by Dr. Taylor and in Bombay by Dr. Lyon, had shown that it contained the acid urate of ammonia, that it was in fact excrementitious; and this year, by opening the cocoons at various intervals, I was able to convince myself of the fact that when the caterpillar has left off feeding and begins to spin it voids the food remaining in the alimentary canal, first of all in a more or less solid form and of a dark colour, but after it has become fully enveloped in the cocoon the excrement comes away as a light-coloured liquid, the hue and consistency of which depend upon the amount of vegetable matter not previously evacuated and the amount of lime, carbon, and ammonia present. The respective proportions of these ingredients vary, I presume, with the food on which the caterpillar has fed and with the state of the atmosphere at the time of spinning, also the longer they remain coating the fibre the harsher and more discoloured it will be. It is therefore very necessary, I think, to remove this cement at a very early date; and this chemistry has shown the manufacturers how to do. Judicious feeding, too, may alter its nature. Before long, fresh cocoons will be at an early stage thoroughly cleansed from all discolouring matter, and Tasar silk will be available for manufacturing purposes as colourless as it is when first put forth by the caterpillar.

"Through the kindness of my correspondent in Sánthal country I have procured a few cocoons of the large or *Chattisghari* variety of the *Tasar* moth, and as this crosses readily with the small or Desi variety which only is found in the Southern Marátha country, I hope next season to procure larger cocoons than I usually do." *

---

* Geoghegan, "Silk Industry of India," p. 111.

The following is extracted from a letter sent to me by J. F. K. Hewitt, Esq., Commissioner, Chota Nagpore, dated September 20th, 1880.

"I shall be exceedingly obliged to you for any information you can give as to the cost of machines for reeling Tusser silk, in order that I may submit a proposition to Government for the introduction of silk reeling as a jail industry, as I thought that if this were proved to be profitable it might give such a stimulus to the cultivation of the Tusser worms as would lead capitalists to lay out the money necessary to make the yield of Tusser from the Highlands of Central India equal to what the country can easily produce with the assistance of capital and organisation. The cost of a machine was a factor necessary to make the system I proposed to Government complete, and I am afraid that in the absence of this information there may be much greater difficulty in having my proposed experiment authorised than there would if I could show clearly the cost on one side of the account and the probable profits on the other.

"I myself can do nothing in the matter beyond laying before Government the probability that by a very little effort a large quantity of Tusser can be produced in the division under my charge, and the very great likelihood of establishing a trade which will conduce to the permanent increase of the wealth of the country, if means can be found to increase the production of Tusser to meet the present growing demand. I must say, however, that Government can never stimulate a trade so quickly as private capital. A much quicker and more easy solution of the difficulty could be worked out by the large silk-houses if they once determined to turn their earnest attention to the subject. Before Tusser silk can be produced on a scale sufficient to meet a really large demand at all approaching to that for China silk, the methods of the trade must be entirely revolutionised. At present Tusser silk is entirely produced by the aboriginal tribes whose villages lie in the valleys running through the hilly country comprised within the circuits of Bhaugulpore, Chota Nagpore, and Cuttack divisions in Bengal, the Chuttisghur, Nagpore, and Jubbulpore divisions in Central India, and in the independent state of Rewa. This country includes an area larger than that of France; and in almost the whole of the hills and forest country, which cover fully three-fifths of its surface, Tusser silk could be profitably produced if the requisite arrangements were made, as the Asun (*Pentaptera tomentosa*), on which the worm thrives best, is found abundantly everywhere. The numbers, however, of the people who cultivate Tusser are small, and these numbers are yearly decreasing as the jungles are cleared and the distance between the village sites and the jungles increases. The cultivator requires that the trees on which the worms are fed should be constantly watched, and superstition adds to the difficulty of the cultivator by insisting that no one can hope to cultivate Tusser worms and reap profit from the cultivation, while maintaining his own health and that of his family, without submitting to a long series of ascetic ordinances during the whole time of watching the worms. If he fails in doing this, the anger of the gods will inevitably destroy him and all belonging to him. As very few of these people will ever consent to live in houses separated by any great distance from their nearest neighbours, it invariably happens that the cultivators find out, as cultivation extends and the area of cleared land between the village and the forest increases, that cultivation is easier and quite as profitable work as Tusser growing with its concomitant annoyances, and so he gives up Tusser and takes to cultivation instead. Of course, if they kept a large number of the Tusser-feeding trees near the village they might contrive both; but this they do not do, as their great object is to get rid of every cover near the village within which wild beasts can hide, and the universal practice, therefore, is to cut down every tree and leave the cultivated land totally unshaded and open. The increase of population, and the yearly increasing area of forest cleared away, therefore tend to lessen the cultivation of Tusser, and it is not possible to increase the production to meet a large demand except by inducing the cultivators to betake themselves to uncleared forests, or else to utilise the partially cleared lands for the cultivation by planting fresh trees and preventing the destruction of those still left. As to the first plan it will be very difficult to carry out, as almost all the best cultivable lands have been already cleared, or are in process of clearance, so that the untouched forests mostly consist of that grown on rocky hill sides where land could not be profitably cultivated. As the means of communication throughout the country are too imperfect to allow of provisions being brought from a distance without the labour of the largest part of the community being used in the transport, it would be impossible at present to make any use of these remote tracts, even if the prejudices of the people as to living on places where they could not grow their favourite crops, where they would have to propitiate strange spirits without the hope of obtaining a permanent settlement by their labours, could be overcome. This last is the most formidable obstacle of all; and though the ideas of the Indian peasant are translated by me into a somewhat illogical form, anyone who knows them will concur with me in saying that this is nothing like so illogical as the reality. This being the case, the only thing to be done is to take up the cultivation systematically; and surely if the future prospects of Tusser are so good as I, and I believe you too, think them to be, it would be worth the while of some of the great houses to send out trustworthy agents to examine the country, select sites for establishing farms on which Tusser could be grown, and devote their energies to superintending the cultivation. By these means the production of Tusser could be largely increased, and cultivation could be extended so as to meet any possible increase of demand. Such an increase is impossible at present, owing to the difficulties stated above, and no largely increased supply can be expected till the whole system is re-organised. If the work be taken in hand, I cannot recommend a more favourable field for experiment than Chota Nagpore. The climate is fairly good, and much cooler than the plains. There is a considerable number of people who are now engaged in the cultivation, and who understand the best methods, and who could be made the means of inducing others to take to the cultivation, providing it were shown to be certain to be profitable; and the trees necessary for rearing the Tusser worm can be found everywhere, and are easily grown and propagated. If you know of any large silkhouses willing to make experiments in this direction, I am sure you cannot use a more effective method of increasing the production of Tusser, and producing a supply commensurate with the increasing demand, than by calling attention to the above statement of facts. I myself shall be very glad to give any information in my power to any large firm wishing to make an organised attempt to increase the production and systematise the cultivation of the silk, as I am sure that no other trade would be of such advantage to the country under my charge."

Mr. Hewitt, in a letter to me dated 19th February 1881, gives me the following particulars regarding the price, &c. of Tusser cocoons :—

"The price of Tusser cocoons, as ascertained by me at Chaibassa in December, the cheapest time of the year, was 8 annas (according to the present rates of exchange, about 10*d.*) per 80 cocoons. Cocoons vary in weight from 50 to the lb. of the newest to 70 to the lb. of the oldest. 1,280 cocoons, not selected according to weight, are calculated to yield about 2 lbs. 6 oz. avoirdupois of silk thread made of from four to five strands, that number of cocoons being all reeled together. This will sell in the bazaar for about 10 rs. 12½ annas, or about 17*s.* according to present rates of exchange."

Captain Brooke says :—

"In Chanda and Sunboolpoor, Central Provinces, while the cocoon crop is gathered, Koshtas, a weaving caste, visit the villages and buy them from the rearers. They are then, as soon as practicable, boiled in a lye made from the ashes of *Jungni* stalks, a plant grown for the oil expressed from its seed. This process effectually kills the chrysalis, at the same time dissolving the mucilage of the cocoon. The cocoons are then stored for use. The method of reeling is primitive in the extreme, and to its imperfections I solely attribute the scant attention this valuable and very beautiful silk has hitherto received. A description of the process is as follows :—The spinner, always a woman, sits on the ground; on her left is an earthen vessel, with a thickish rim, about six inches in diameter and three inches deep. The saucer is three parts filled with a mixture of potash and ashes patted down to a level surface, and kept damp with water. Upon this the cocoons to be spun are placed, the outer portion, of inferior and nearly useless silk, having been first removed. The thread in ordinary use among the weavers is spun from seven cocoons; these are all placed at the same time in the earthen saucer; a filament is then taken up from each cocoon, and, being brought together, are rolled between the hand and left thigh of the spinner, which are kept damp by an acid solution of tamarind and water."

In Bengal the cocoons are put into boiling water to kill the pupæ; in some districts, when intended for sale, they are put in boiling water and dried in the sun. In the Nizam's country the cocoons are loaded with dhobee's earth and alkaline ashes to make them reel. In the Midnapoor district they are boiled in cowdung and reeled by hand.

Captain Brooke says that in Seonee the pierced cocoons are wound, and that no koshtee rejects a cocoon simply because the moth has eaten its way through it. He has fallen into an error in stating the moth's mode of exit from its cocoon. It does not eat its way out, but separates the fibres with its legs and wing spine, and so creeps out. It has neither teeth nor mouth proper.

Each species of silkworm has two stores of silk, one on each side of the alimentary canal, and below its mouth it has two so-called spinnarets or orifices, through which the silk issues simultaneously in fine parallel filaments. As the silk is drawn out of the stores, the worm coats it with a varnish technically called gum, which contains a brownish-yellow colouring matter.

The *Tusser* worm, in spinning its cocoon, takes short sweeps of its head from side to side, depositing the silk very closely in parallel fibres, which take a zigzag course round the cocoon as he does so. It has been thought that the worm twists or spins the silk as it exudes it, but this is not the case. Besides the gum which coats the silk, the worm secretes at intervals a cementing fluid, which it kneads by an expanding motion of its body through the whole cocoon to consolidate and harden it. This cement gives to the cocoon its drab colour.

There is a striking peculiarity about the fibre of Tusser silk. I have carefully and thoroughly examined it many times under the microscope, and find undoubtedly that it is almost flat (Plate XXVIII., Figs 3 and 4), and not round, as is the case in the silk produced by the mulberry-fed worm *Bombyx mori* (Plate XXVIII., Figs. 1 and 2).

There is no doubt that it is to this property that Tusser silk owes its glassy or vitreous look, reflecting a little glare of light from the angle of incidence on its flat surface, whilst the mulberry-silk fibre, being round, reflects the light in all directions.

By some this property is considered a drawback, but by the time the fibre has become modified and the flatness diffused in the loom I think the lustre of the cloth is enhanced by it.

This tape-like appearance gives the fibre this disadvantage, that it is less homogeneous than the round fibre of the mulberry silk, and I find an undoubted tendency in it to split up into smaller fibrets, of which the fibre is evidently composed, causing the silk to swell out when subjected to severe dyeing processes, particularly the bleaching one of recent date, thus giving a substantial and important reason why its coloured cements should be removed, if possible, by gentle action. The natural colour of Tusser silk is a darkish shade of fawn, much unlike the golden and white colours of mulberry silk.

The fibrets have a distinct structure, upwards of 20 in number, composing each fibre, and seem compactly laid together, showing longitudinal striæ under the microscope (Plate XXVIII., Fig. 4). I conceive it is this fibrous compound structure, absent in the mulberry fibre (Plate XXVIII., Fig. 2), which is an element in its dye-resisting power. I found permanganate of potash to be the best agent to separate these fibrets.

The diameter, from edge to edge, of a single flat fibre of Tusser from the outer part of the cocoon averages $\frac{1}{770}$ part of an inch, and from deeper in the substance of the cocoon $\frac{1}{710}$ of an inch, but the external fibres are much more variable than the internal ones. The thickness from side to side is $\frac{1}{1900}$ of an inch. The outside fibres are capable of supporting without breaking an average weight of seven drams, and the inner eight drams, whilst the usual amount of tension before breaking in all the fibres is one inch to the foot (*see* table, page 68). The fibres, like all other silk fibres, are laid in the cocoon by the silkworm in pairs, and are, like all flat silk fibres, united by their edges, and not by their flat surfaces.

All the *Saturniidæ* fibres I have examined are more or less striated and composed of fibrets, and are flattish, except the English species, *Saturnia carpini*, or *Emperor* moth (Plate XXI., Figs. 1 and 2), which in North Staffordshire spins a beautiful cocoon in the heather of our moorlands. Plate XXIX., Fig. 6, is an enlarged microscopic appearance of this silk, which shows its transparent and fibreless nature; and also, what is very curious, that the fibres are round except when they come in contact with each other, when they become flat; no doubt, from pressure whilst the fibres were in their fresh viscous state. This apparent exception to the *Saturniidæ* depositing flat fibres, and the *Bombycidæ* round ones, which I had established, possibly points to the secretion of the sericine in the different species, varying in viscidity, that of the *Saturniidæ* being secreted in a more fluid state than in that of the *Bombycidæ*. There may also be a difference in the structure of their seripositors; but this I have not had at present an opportunity of investigating.

It is a fallacy, held by some entomologists, that the worm in all species, both *Bombycidæ* and *Saturniidæ*, twists or spins the two threads together as it forms them at the orifice of its spinnarets. The two threads are simply laid side by side. It would be impossible to twist the two threads without the worm itself revolving continuously with the emission of the silk, or having spinning wheels at the secreting orifice. I propose, therefore, to change the word "spinnaret," which conveys an inaccurate impression, and substitute for it that of "seripositor."

CHAPTER VI.

New and Improved Processes of Reeling, Spinning, Dyeing, and Printing Tusser Silk, with Account of its Uses.

Leaving now the more beaten track of the natural history side of the question, I come to speak of its merchantable and art side.

In 1874 I had the honour to receive a communication from Sir Louis Mallet, Under Secretary of State for India, asking me to communicate, "for the information of the " Government of India, any details I might be in a position " to furnish on the subject of dyeing the wild silk pro- " duced by the *Tusser* worm."

On my report being received I was requested to make a full investigation of the subject, which divided itself naturally into two heads—a consideration of the silk, and of tinctorial matters. For the first, I found the raw Tusser silk as it comes into this country to be prepared by the natives of India and China in such a rude and filthy state as to interpose unnecessary obstacles to its taking the dyes. I felt sure that cleaner and more skilful methods of reeling and preparing the silk for the market would be accompanied by less resistance to tinctorial matter, as well as furnishing a greatly improved quality. At my request, orders were issued for the collection in the different provinces of India of a complete assortment of native dyestuffs as well as a complete supply of Tusser silk.

In recommending the Government of India to have the natives taught the dyeing of their wild silks with dyestuffs indigenous to India, I had two motives, one to prevent the native art of India being tampered with by the introduction of European fugitive dyes and crude colours, and another that they could be made to utilise that in which their country has ever been so rich, the remarkable variety of native-grown dyestuffs which in other than wild silk fabrics they have known probably for thousands of years so well how to use. To take dyestuffs to India must surely be carrying coals to Newcastle. I have since received an extensive and most interesting series of India dyestuffs and tanning materials, which I have at present under examination. Some of these native dyestuffs, with proper mordants, give much more permanent colours than the fugitive aniline dyes the use of which for artistic purposes and for goods intended to last a long time cannot be too seriously lamented. They are suitable only for dyes intended for short use. My examination already promises well. I have succeeded in applying several dyes to Tusser silk which seem to possess the desirable merit of permanence, and no doubt others will also impart colours to the silk with satisfactory results when I have found suitable mordants for them. I also received a quantity of Tusser cocoons, and, not being able to have them reeled in England, I was authorised to go to Italy to see if I could have them reeled there, and effect my hope for improvement in the manufacture. By the introduction of a friend, I obtained permission to visit one of the filatures in Piedmont, at St. Cio, near Torre Pellice. On arriving there I found an extensive mulberry-silk reeling and throwing establishment, situated in a most beautiful valley, in one of the southern spurs of the Alps, about three hours' journey north of Turin.

On explaining my mission, and showing the wild cocoons, I was told there was not much prospect of success, for several trials had been made, and they had been found difficult to soften and impracticable to work; but knowing too well how natural is the tendency to look at objections rather than at the means when any new idea presents itself, and feeling too that the difficulties might be resolved, I asked to be allowed to try myself. The permission being generously granted, and every assistance kindly afforded me, I was taken to the reeling room, where about 100 young women were at work, with well-trained fingers, reeling the small Piedmont cocoons of *Bombyx mori*. The operation was interesting in the extreme, heightened as it was by their strange singing of old French songs, in a dialect not even understood by the Italians, a strange and all but forgotten tongue, which has to be learned by the mill-overlookers before they can communicate their instructions to them. I was told these girls were the descendants of Huguenot refugees, escaped probably from Provence to the Italian side of the Alps at the Revocation of the Edict of Nantes, and that they still retained their patois and their folk lore; they worked hard for the few months of cocoon reeling, from five in the morning until eight at night, for a franc a day; after work dancing and singing for the hour before bed time in the most joyous way. Apartments are provided for them at the factory, and when the reeling season is over they separate and return to their Alpine villages, to wait for the next season's work.

The operation of unwinding the silk from the cocoon is as follows:—A number of cocoons are immersed in an iron pan, in water nearly boiling, with a little alkali to soften them. A semi-rotating brush is placed over them, which quickly catches the exterior fibres of each cocoon, and the more readily enables the reeler to find the windable thread. They are then taken out and transferred to the reeler, who sits leaning over an iron pan of about 12 inches in diameter in which she has a few cocoons in hot water, the found ends of several being in one hand. Four or six cocoons, as the case may be, are being simultaneously reeled into a single thread by the reel at her back, which draws off over her head the cocoon threads while the cocoons are dancing and turning in the water. When a thread breaks, or the cocoon is reeled, another is quickly presented from the lot in the other hand, the manipulation being one of great dexterity. Several years are required to attain proficiency, and it is not until the fifth to the seventh year that a reeler is entrusted with the most delicate reeling; the keeping of the size of the thread regular and free from rough places being the most important care.

It is this branch of the manufacture that in Tusser silk is so defectively treated in India. The native mode of reeling the thread of silk from the cocoon is by the implements represented in Plate LVI.; this shows how rudely the manipulation is managed as compared to the more finished reeling appliance of the Italians. In some instances the silk is reeled from the cocoon round the naked knee-cap of the reeler.

I took some of my wild cocoons, and, with much difficulty and patience, after several trials, succeeded in softening them by the aid of long-continued boiling in water, to which were added soap, potash, and glycerine. When soft enough, one of the most skilled girls was told off to reel them for me, and, after ridding the cocoons of the outer and coarser threads, she reeled the thread of four cocoons into one, almost without a break, much to her own delight and to the surprise of my friends and myself.

The next day, the resulting Tusser raw silk was taken to the throwing mill, and there made into Organzine and Tram, of such fineness as to surprise my friends, who said they had no idea that Tusser silk could be made of so fine a thread, and that they should think seriously about sending a person to India to collect Tusser cocoons, that their work-people might wind them after their mulberry crop had been finished.

The usual size—that is, thickness—of thread of thrown Tusser silk of commerce was, up to this time, 152 to 255 deniers; that is, skeins, of 1,000 yards long, weighing 9 to 15 drams. From some of the finer raw silk a size of 6 to 7 drams was obtained, but it was generally coarser. From the cocoons the reeling of which I superintended I obtained a size of 51 deniers, or three drams, per 1,000 yards. (*See* No. 15 in the collection.)

In 1878 I met M. H. Meyer, a silk manufacturer at Milan and one of my colleagues in the silk jury at the Paris Exhibition. He took much interest in my work and its results. From cocoons I afterwards sent him he obtained raw silk of 23–27 deniers, or 1½ drams, per 1,000 yards. From this he produced Organzine and Tram (warp and weft threads) of 50 to 55 deniers or 3 drams, results agreeing with my own; which are also in the collection. He found some of my cocoons very difficult to reel, no doubt owing to their age, and to not having been reeled before weather exposure. Fourteen pounds and a half yielded one pound of raw silk. He informs me that some cocoons he has just purchased in Marseilles were larger in size than those I sent him; they are darker in colour, but reel much better. He is obtaining from ten pounds of them one pound of raw silk.

Even a finer thread might be obtained; but as the fibre is only the $\frac{1}{710}$th part of an inch, or three times as thick as ordinary silk, I think 51 deniers is a good and practicable limit when native reelers can have proper appliances, and be taught to be as handy as the reelers of Italy or the south of France. I daresay some of my readers may remember the improvements which took place in reeling the mulberry silks of Bengal and Brutia, when superior skill and machinery were introduced, a good many years ago. Before that time, Bengal silks were held in very low estimation, and were very difficult to work, but after the introduction of better appliances Bengal silks were shown to be as capable of refinement as any other; and Brutia silk now commands, by its superior quality, the highest price in the market; and I have no doubt that, in degree, equal success lies waiting for the Tusser-silk industry.

I trust I may point to this manufacturing development and great improvement with pardonable pride, more especially as I am not a manufacturer, and could scarcely expect to find untrodden ground in a domain distinct from, although allied to, my own.

The new-reeled silk is much lighter in colour than native-reeled, and has very much more lustre; in fact, it is the most lustrous in the undyed state of all silks, and possesses greater strength. I found, what I expected to find, that the silk thus reeled dyes much more easily; more shades and lighter ones can be dyed upon it than native-reeled; it has no disagreeable smell, and only loses two ounces per pound in being cleaned for dyeing, where native-reeled Tusser loses in some cases as much as six to seven ounces per pound, and never less than four to five ounces. It is as clean, to use a technical term, which means free from "slubs" and irregularities of thread, as ordinary silk. The cost of reeling new and good cocoons, and manufacturing them into Organzine and Tram, is about seven shillings per pound; but it would be less when the collection and storing of the cocoons is better understood, and the chrysalis more carefully killed. It is making way, both all silk and in mixtures, in many fabrics where extreme fineness is not required, and for a variety of purposes, in passementerie, trimmings, braids, scarves, broad, and narrow goods. It is now considerably used for these purposes in France. Its price has gradually risen, whilst that of other silks has either remained stationary or actually depreciated.

I have urged on the Government of India the importance of introducing to the natives of India the European modes of reeling cocoons, and some time ago drew their attention to an invention which simplifies and economises this operation.

Mr. Mackenzie, engineer, of Milan, has introduced a Milan house of filateurs, who have invented and patented another mode of reeling, by which skilled labour is dispensed with. If this machine is pronounced by experts to be a success, there is no reason why cocoon reeling should not be carried on in any village home, as flax spinning was formerly. Should this machine be found to be unsuitable, there is no doubt the ordinary reeling appliances of Italy and the South of France would leave nothing to be desired in effectively and economically reeling the Tusser cocoons.*

M. David, the largest ribbon manufacturer in St. Etienne, seeing this improved manufacture and dyeing in the Indian section of the Paris Exhibition, where they were first displayed, offered to buy all the cocoons produced in India, if the price would not be more than one franc per kilogramme. He has applied to the India Government for 2,000 kilogrammes of cocoons for experiments at his own cost. It would be a very good thing for a trade to spring up in Tusser cocoons. The natives could easily be encouraged to breed a larger supply, whilst improvements in reeling would require time, and would meet with obstacles of race, religion, and habit difficult to overcome; the enterprise in this direction would have to be purely private and mercantile, as I think the Government of India would not enter into commercial undertakings, but would probably, and certainly ought to, give most strenuous encouragement and help to stimulate the further spread of this most interesting industry.

I was requested by Dr. Birdwood, in 1878, to show, in the Indian section of the Paris Exhibition, the developments of which Tusser silk was capable. He placed me in communication with Sir P. Cunliffe Owen, K.C.M.G., C.B., who entered most warmly into the idea, and took the greatest interest in it throughout, giving me all the encouragement and help required to make the collection worthy of being represented side by side with the beautiful objects from India, worthy of the traditions of the gorgeous East. It was the India of the artist which asserted itself at Paris—the old historic land, from which art manufactures in brocades, printed calicoes, jewellery, ivory carving, and pottery may still draw their highest aspirations.

In the wild-silk exhibits which I have been requested to bring together in the new India section of the South Kensington Museum are shown, not only the improvements in manufacturing and dyeing of which I have spoken, but another and more decorative phase, and one developed, so far as I can gather, for the first time in the history of

* This machine has been recently much improved and patented. It will shortly be brought to England for inspection, the inventor having sanguine hopes of a very extended use for it in the silk-reeling districts of Asia and Europe, both for reeling mulberry and Tusser silks. It will now produce a larger quantity and will yield a perfectly classical silk.

either the East or West—that of printing. It had struck me that fabrics made of Tusser silk, either of native or home manufacture, would be susceptible of much enrichment if they could be printed upon. After many fruitless attempts, at a considerable outlay, I at last succeeded, and since that time I have had the satisfaction of applying and fixing a much wider range of colours.

Thinking that designs of an Eastern type were naturally the most applicable to cloths of this wild silk, I obtained, by the courtesy of Dr. Forbes Watson, the loan of a large series of wood-printing blocks, of native design and workmanship, from the old India Museum. I have used these for many of the printed illustrations in the collection, and have consistently adhered to the use of Indian colours. The designs on these blocks are exceedingly interesting, as will be seen in Plate LV. In England the finer details would be of copper, but in these they are of the hardest wood, and the details of the pattern most skilfully cut.

Since the results of my developments were exhibited at the Paris Exhibition of 1878, Tusser silks have been largely printed and worn both in France and England. Printed pompadours on Tusser have since been very fashionable. These printed silks can be successfully used for wall damasks, curtains, furniture coverings, hangings, and women's and girls' dresses with excellent effect; and I would call the attention of upholsterers and broad-silk manufacturers to the specimens in the collection in the India section. The silk fabrics made of Tusser are very strong, most durable, and possess much lustre. I have pointed out at p. 68 the superior strength of Tusser to ordinary silk, it being between three and four times greater than that of *Bombyx mori*.

There will be found in the collection a series of patterns, No. 87, which, by the kindness of Messrs. Clayton, Marsdens, Holden, & Co., who prepared them, I am enabled to exhibit, showing to what uses the waste of Tusser silk and the cocoons pierced by the exit of the moth can be put by spinning in the same way as threads of cotton and wool are manufactured. It commences with samples of pierced cocoons which could not be wound, and waste silk from ordinary Tusser manufacture, followed by samples showing the various processes the silk undergoes before it is made into thread or cord for weaving or for sewing purposes. This series of patterns will be found described in order in the catalogue at the end of this manual.

This suggests forcibly a promising economy in store for the produce of all silk-making worms. There are many species unknown to commerce, rejected because of their not being capable of being reeled or wound in the ordinary way; but now that spinning machinery is in such a perfected state, all cocoons and waste silk may be spun and converted into materials of some use or other.

In Simla alone there are said to be eight or nine species of *Bombyx*, which, no doubt, might be utilised in this way as well as many, if not all, the species enumerated in Mr. Moore's list at p. 3. I strongly recommend that all the waste of Tusser be collected; the outer part of the cocoon, being removed by the native reeler, should be put aside for this purpose. It is only practicable to obtain one pound of reeled silk from 11 lbs. of cocoons minus their chrysalides, and the remaining 10 lbs. of waste is eagerly sought after by the European spinners.

Messrs. Clayton, Marsdens, Holden, & Co., silk spinners of Halifax, have made for me several beautiful specimens of fabrics woven in different designs from pierced cocoons and waste Tusser, with which I furnished them from material collected for me in India by the order of Her Majesty's Government of India. They have been successful in perfecting to a surprising degree the manufacture of fabric from Tusser-silk waste, which a few years ago could not find buyers at 4*d.* per lb., and which lay about the English ports for some time quite unsaleable. So much is it now in demand that it is worth 2*s.* per lb. I also mention the successful weaving of reeled Tusser by Messrs. J. Birchenough & Sons, of Macclesfield, who have made in this branch a special effort of late years. Messrs. Brocklehurst & Co., Messrs. Smale, Bros., and a few other Macclesfield manufacturers, have also recently helped to develop this industry.

Considerable quantities of Tusser silk have also been manufactured in France by manufacturers unknown to me, and not a little has been used in France and England for the black gauffred braids so much worn of late for fringe; they have been almost as effective as mulberry-silk braids.

In March 1878 there were nearly 2,000 bales of Tusser raw silk in London that could not find buyers even at so low a price as from 2*s.* 3*d.* to 2*s.* 9*d.* per lb., organzine and tram being at that time 3*s.* 6*d.* to 4*s.* 6*d.* per lb., whilst at the present time there is scarcely a bale to be bought in the market, and the value of Tusser raw has risen to not less than 7*s.* to 9*s.* per lb. Notwithstanding a long depression in the silk trade, which has caused mulberry silk to decrease in value, Tusser silk has steadily increased to its present rates. I attribute this remarkable change in the value of Tusser silk partly to the fact of the discovery of the successful application of colour by dyeing and printing to this silk, hitherto so intractable and dye-resisting, and partly to the immense improvements which have taken place in its manufacture and applications.

Owing to my successful experiment in Italy in 1876 for the Government of India, showing the susceptibility of even so coarse a fibre as Tusser being reeled into yarn of 52 deniers, the idea has since been carried out in practice by the Italian manufacturers to some extent, and cocoons have been imported and reeled and thrown there. The present price of improved reeled Tussar in Italy is now 3½ to 4 times the price of ordinary native-reeled. I have lately been receiving samples of beautifully reeled silk from thence, and marked at the following prices:—

	deniers.		*s.*	*d.*				
Organzine	40·44	–	21	11	per lb.	No.	2	Sample
Tram	- 40·44	–	18	2	„	„	3	„
Raw	- 20·22	–	14	7	„	„	1	„

I consider these prices above the intrinsic value of Tusser silk; but if better arrangements were made for collecting the cocoons in India, the silk might be purchased at much lower prices, and lower still if the improved reeling appliances of Italy could be taken to India, where labour is so much cheaper and time of so much less value.

These excessive prices are still more remarkable at a time when the best silks of commerce are extraordinarily low in price.

The uses of Tusser silk are rapidly increasing. My spinners tell me that such are their orders for Tusser schappe, *i.e.*, spun Tusser silk, that, large as their mill now is, they would increase it threefold could they obtain an adequate supply of raw material. They have recently bought 25,000 lbs. to 30,000 lbs. of Tusser waste, and would contract for 30,000 lbs. more if supply were available. The price they are now paying is 2*s.* per lb. either for cocoons or waste. They have even been carding and spinning reeled Tusser silk which they bought when Tusser raws were low.

One of the most important uses to which Tusser silk has yet been applied is in the manufacture, first accomplished in 1880 in England, of the fabric known as "Seal cloth," which consists of a Tusser silk plush woven into a cotton back.

The use of this fabric for cloaks and mantles for ladies, winter wear offers a considerable advantage over the use of sealskin, from its intended resemblance to which it has derived its name, in that, having a woven back, it is perfectly porous. Tusser silk is peculiarly adapted for this manufacture, owing to its beautiful soft feel and lustrous appearance, and to the fact that its fibre, being three times as thick as mulberry silk, offers sufficient resistance to pressure which would otherwise disarrange the fibres of such long plush, which lie regularly, just as in sealskin.

Seal cloth has a most rich appearance, and easily recovers injury from wet or pressure by simply being placed before the fire and then brushed. Tusser silk for this manufacture is spun into yarn, and not reeled from the cocoon, and its application to this purpose is now becoming very extensive.

Extensive orders are in contract for the winter season in brown and a variety of colours; the beautiful soft feel of the plush is sure to make it a favourite material.

Owing to private arrangements of the manufacturers with the merchants, who are not desirous that the material should be exhibited at present, I am unable to obtain specimens for the Museum, but by the time the Handbook is published there will be ample opportunity to secure some. It is likely to be the most useful and fashionable stuff for cloaks and mantles for the winter, and, having a woven back, will be porous, and not liable to the objections of seal or other skins. The pile is made to lie exactly as in sealskin.

It also bids fair to become a rival if not a substitute for Utrecht velvet; it has a marked adaptability to the purpose for which this velvet is used, having a softer pile and much more brilliancy. It is destined, for this use particularly, to a permanent future unaffected by the fluctuations of fashion.

I am glad to announce that I have found a new use for Tusser silk: it will be found eminently applicable for making silk carpets and rugs, for this reason, that its fibre is three times thicker than the silk of commerce, making therefore a better and firmer pile. A sample which I have had made promises the best results.

It is also coming into extensive use for travelling rugs

alone and for woven tapestries of mixed materials. The lustre of the silk enlivens up the effect in a very pleasing manner.

Another use which I have also found for it is its insertion in tailoring cloths for brightening up the effect.

I have placed in the collection a specimen of plush made with Tusser organzine (No. 43 of the collection), which I believe to be as superior in firmness of pile to the silk carpets of India as the carpets of thicker wools and camels' hair are to those made from very fine wools.

The following India-made carpets of silk are now exhibited in the New India section at the South Kensington Museum :—

One from Malabar, modern.
One from Wurungal, 16th century.
One Mongolian, 18th century.
One place not named, 18th century.
One silk and cotton carpet.
One from Hyderabad, Deccan.

Beautiful as they are, particularly the older ones, the pile in each is inferior to the accompanying Tusser specimen of plush ; and I wish to emphasise this superiority in order to draw the attention of carpet manufacturers to the important and not too well-known fact that a stiff fibre is generally better than a fine one for carpet work, and that Tusser silk accordingly is better than mulberry silk for the purpose, whilst, in addition, it will not be possible to vulgarise the effects of colour to so great an extent as may be seen in most carpet-shop windows, because of the difficulty and cost of dyeing Tusser silk into very pale shades, and also that Tusser silk properly dyed inherently takes shades of artistic merit.

The artistic effects will be correspondingly better with the increased firmness of the staple, its greater durability, and less liability of flattening by pressure and wear.

Tusser silk, both reeled and spun (and I hope my non-manufacturing readers will by this time have recognised the difference in manufacture between reeled silk and spun, *i.e.*, carded and spun, silk), is being extensively used for making mantle stuffs in imitation of and a substitute for sealskin. I have no doubt that spun Tusser will also prove to be applicable to carpet weaving as well as the *reeled* Tusser described above, whilst, from the probability of its being of lower value if quantities can be produced, it will be employed in the production of low-priced carpets. The present price, however, of Tusser spun yarn is 11*s.* per lb., actually greater, on account of the present large demand, than Tusser organzine and tram made of native-reeled raw, which can be bought at 7*s.* 6*d.* to 10*s.* per lb.

Thus, for both Indian and English silk-carpet weaving, a new application lies open, as well as other uses now being developed. As far as my examination has been able to extend, I have not found in the immense collection of native-dyed silks of all kinds of manufacture, artistic or industrial, in the New Indian Museum, any specimens of dyed Tusser silk except in the new collection of Indian wild silk which I have had the honour to prepare and arrange there.

In addition to the fabrics before mentioned, Tusser silk is used for the manufacture of beautiful woven cloths, which are styled grenadine or mandarin.

Had the people of India been able to have had Tusser silk dyed into their artistic colours, no doubt this silk would have been utilised for carpets and other kinds of art and industrial coloured work.

I much regret that, owing to the superior quickness of the Chinese, they are trying to supply the present demand, and most of the Tusser waste and raw silk now finding its way to England is from China. It behoves, therefore, every one interested in India, both in governing and trading there, to open up the produce of a country in which this silk is so widespread.

The following table shows the state of the London market in Tusser silk for the last few years and the remarkably increased consumption since the Paris Exhibition of 1878.—

Year.	Stock, Jan. 1st.	Imported.	Consumed.
	Bales.	Bales.	Bales.
1874	662	none.	168
1875	494	none.	319
1876	175	427	174
1877	428	1,037	284
1878	1,181	837	736
1879	1,282	58	1,142
1880	194	—	—

The average consumption for the four years ending 1877 was 238 bales, whilst the consumption for 1878, the year that attention was drawn to it by the Paris exhibits, more than trebled itself, the purchases being, as will be seen in the above table, 736 bales for that year. For 1879 the consumption was still more surprising, being 1,142 bales.

The imports of Tusser silk and Tusser silk waste into Marseilles since the commencement of 1879 are as follows:

During 1876, 1877, and 1878 are unknown.

1879,	53 bales of silk.		
	59	„	waste.
1880,	347	„	silk.
	147	„	waste.

For the first three months of 1881, 144 bales of silk.
22 „ waste.

M. V. Bizot, of the firm of Messrs. Arlès, Dufour, & Cie., of Lyons, to whom I am indebted for these particulars, thinks the figures for 1879 are probably too small; but he has no means of controlling them.

This table shows an enormous increase in France in the consumption of Tusser silk. If the figures for 1879 are correct, it will be seen that during the year 1880 nearly 4½ times as much of this silk was imported as during 1879; and the first three months of 1881 show a still greater increase.

The following table shows the prices of silks of commerce and Tusser in the London market for April 1879:—

	s.	*d.*
China raw tsatlee, No. 4, per lb. - -	15	6
Canton „ „ 1, „ - - -	13	6
„ „ „ 4, „ - -	11	6
Japan raw marbush, No. 2½, per lb. - -	16	0
Italian organzine - - - -	25	0
Bengal raw - - - - - - - -	14	6
Brutia „ - - - - -	23	0
Tusser „ - - - 4*s.* 6*d.* to	5	3

Tusser raw has since gradually advanced, the price being now from 7*s.* 6*d.* to 10*s.*, according to quality, as I have previously shown.

Dyeing of Tusser.

A good deal is beginning to be said as to the rival merits and demerits of aniline dyes and those of older and more permanent natures. The advocates of each probably allow their prejudices or preference to guide their conclusion beyond what can be borne out by either history or practice.

It is perfectly true that the older modes of dyeing generally gave more permanent results than the modern modes.

That is an incontrovertible fact, and one need not stop to cite instances to prove it.

Old specimens of woven fabrics of silk may be seen in the South Kensington Museum, whose colours have stood, but little impaired, for more centuries than the results of modern dyes would stand months of exposure to light.

It is also as true that the dyes from aniline, napthalymine, and other kindred derivatives are fugitive, and it is exceedingly improbable that science will ever make them proof against that most searching and crucical of all tests—light.

The natural hues of colour of the older modes of dyeing and their combinations are also of more refined and therefore more artistic tones than the modern chemical dyes give ; hence they are preferred by those whose tastes and insight are more artistic than those of the general public, which are more or less unrefined, and therefore more or less meretricious and gaudy.

But a remarkable change has gradually come over the preference for colour throughout Europe within the last 20 years, or since the days when the magenta colour was adored. Less gaudy colours are now preferred in all decorative departments, and the truer principles of colour combinations are more understood and liked. There can be no doubt this change has been brought about, in painting for instance, by modern pre-Raphael thought and work.

So much has this influence been felt, consciously and unconsciously, that the colour products for the million, recently and even now occasionally so gaudy, have given way to more sober hues and combinations. As the whole of the colour in modern commerce in dyeing and printing is produced, practically so to speak, by aniline and analogous dyes, it has been found comparatively simple to imitate and produce the more sober hues by the admixture in varying proportions of these chemical dyes, not, it is true, so perfectly as to prevent detection by the skilled eye, or more effectually by laboratory tests, but sufficiently so as to subdue the garish effects I have mentioned.

Hence, it may be argued, are aniline dyes to be totally condemned?

Much as we justly condemn in the aniline dyes all that is so garish and so fugitive, we are led to the consideration of the controversy of to-day as to whether we may legitimately use aniline dyes, or, in fact, any fugitive dyes, and their combined coloured effects, or not.

I do not wish to be an apologist for fugitive dyes, whether the source be aniline or not, but in fairness I ought not to omit to put on record in this argument that, in practice, there have always been the two kinds of dyeing, viz., permanent and fugitive and that each has its use.

No one can read an old French work on dyeing without constantly meeting with the phrases *bon teint* (fast dye) and *petit teint* (fugitive dye). They were always produced to order by any dyer, but for different purposes. In the East, too, where for thousands of years the best dyeing has been done, has the same practice prevailed, and the fugitive dyes have been used, but, it is true, to a more limited extent than the permanent ones.

Having been engaged for some years in the examination of both the dyed fabrics and the dyestuffs of India, I can truly state that several of the dyestuffs of vegetable origin are extremely fugitive; yet they have long been and are still used there.

There are many purposes for which the cheaper and more speedily applied fugitive dyes may be used, and will always be used so long as they are more economical in either saving money or time, as, for example, all fabrics which are not designed or intended to last long or to wear long or to be exposed to sunlight.

I may mention two of the most useful dyes, without which dyers all over the world would find it difficult to match the patterns of their clients, neither of which are of aniline origin. I allude to turmeric, an Indian dye, (the root of *Curcuma longa*,) and the sulphate of indigo. The first I have been surprised to find to be the dye of the brilliant yellows of some of the garments of India and Kashgar, and it is even more fugitive than many of the aniline dyes to both light and chemical re-agents. Sulphate of indigo, whilst being fairly fast to light, disappears with washing, and should never be used for any fabric that has to be afterwards wetted or soaped.

But whilst having written so much for the aniline side of the question, I must not be supposed to waver in my allegiance to *bon teint*, and I unhesitatingly say that modern dyeing and printing is in a very discreditable and unsatisfactory condition, and the fugitive dyes are mainly used for purposes where a more rigid conscientiousness on the part of the manufacturers would never permit their use. It is no fault of the dyer; he provides either *petit teint* or *bon teint*, at the desire of his customer the fabricant, perhaps not to order always, but certainly to price, and often very low price; and inasmuch as *petit teint* is cheaper and more quickly applied, materials are dyed by modes which cannot be too emphatically condemned, nor is the manufacturer or merchant to be altogether blamed for this debased state of things.

For by far the most purposes of life to which colour is found to be a necessity and a comfort, the quality of permanence is imperative, as well as that such colour should partake of that sobriety and refinement which distinguishes art from meretricious imitation of it.

Amongst these may be mentioned all kinds of furniture and upholstery decorations, carpets, printed fabrics, and so much of dress as the tyranny of a frequent changing fashion will allow.

The best modes of imparting colour to the wild silks of India have for some time engaged my attention, at the request of the Government of India.

With regard to the Eria and Mooga silks the investigations are yet too incomplete for me to state more than I have done under their respective headings, pp. 53, 61.

I will describe as briefly as I can some of the more salient points in my recent experiences and developments of dyeing Tusser silk.

Finding, many years ago, that Tusser silk opposed a resistance in no ordinary degree to tinctorial matter, I took an interest in the subject with a view of overcoming this resistance.

In its small affinity, ordinarily speaking, for colouring matter, it ranks with the vegetable fibres of cotton and flax; and whilst, in many processes, it would come out scarcely tinted, the mulberry-bred silk would be found to have seized the colour with avidity. It, however, takes the aniline dyes, under certain conditions, moderately well. At that time, and for some years previously, little Tusser silk had passed through the dye-houses. About 40 years ago an attempt was made to introduce it in Macclesfield for sewing silk for black; but, on account of its irregular way of taking the dye, it was abandoned, with the result that little or no Tusser silk has been used for sewing purposes from that day to this. About 12 years ago I made many experiments in dyeing this silk, and had the satisfaction of seeing my way to further improvement.

In 1873, the firm of which I am senior partner, consisting of my brother and myself, exhibited, at the International Exhibition at South Kensington, the result of progress up to that time in a series of black and coloured silks, which were in advance of any similar effort, either English or continental, as far as my observations or knowledge extended, and they attracted a good deal of attention, and led to a further utilisation of Tusser silk, then a drug in the market, except for dress silks for women and girls in the undyed and pleasing shade natural to it, which is fawn colour.

The development up to that time had been that this silk could be dyed into any middle or dark shade of drab, slate, brown, green, violet, or dark red, whilst to pale shades of blues, pinks, cerise, scarlet, and others the dark natural ground colour of the silk interposed an insuperable barrier, as sulphur, or any then known bleaching agent, could not reduce the silk to a whiter state.

The desideratum of pale shades led our quick French neighbours to study the composition of the brown-colouring matter, and to find a solvent for it. The credit of this achievement must be awarded to the late M. Tessié du Motay, who was led to try permanganate of potash, which was at that time attracting much attention on account of its great oxidising power on organic matter. He found the browny colorant yielded to this agent. Unfortunately, the oxidising action being too violent, the fibre of the silk as well as its coloration was affected, and by the time it became white enough for dyeing into pale colours the silk was rendered useless. However, a secret had been discovered; and it was this, that oxygen, under certain combining conditions, united with the colouring matter, which then became separated from the silk.

The object now was to apply the oxygen under gentler conditions. This M. Tessié du Motay again succeeded in doing, and in a very ingenious way. He brought into contact with the silk an insoluble body; this, on contact, should yield up an atom of oxygen, in the nascent form, which should gently unite with the fawn-coloured matter of the silk without attacking the fibre. This, although a rough method, solved the difficulty, and the silk can now be bleached so as to have a sufficiently pale ground to admit of its being dyed into any pale colour except white.

The substance he found to comply with the required condition is binoxide of barium. Unfortunately, the process is expensive. It costs almost 2*s*. per lb. to use and apply it. This, in addition to the cost of dyeing, prevents its being used as extensively as it would be if it were as cheap as the mode of bleaching ordinary silk, which is by sulphurous acid; but there is a probability of the principle being shortly applied by other methods which will be at the same time cheaper and more within the legitimate sphere of dye-house technical operation than that of M. Tessié du Motay; I mean, whereby the nascent oxygen shall be presented to the silk in the vat from a solution, instead of from a solid, as at present.

Major Coussmaker has succeeded in obtaining perfectly white Tusser silk by alteration of the conditions under which the worm spins its cocoons He causes the caterpillar to void all its cement before allowing it to spin its cocoon, but he does not give full particulars of his method. His experiment is very remarkable. He has sent me a cocoon which is free from all brownness, and resembles the Chinese or Japanese cocoons in shade. If this result is attainable, the difficult and costly bleaching process will be rendered unnecessary. It would be curious and useful to know if so desirable a result is practicable.

For all darkish shades I have found aniline dyes the most effective, and in some cases the only, way at present of obtaining them; and until effective modes of dyeing Tusser silk into permanent dark shades are discovered, *petit teint* must be employed for them as also for the lighter shades for commercial uses.

The artistic demand alone is not sufficient to stimulate a growing industry like this, nor to encourage the utilisation of a product which can be cultivated over nearly the whole of India; and it is better to use what lies ready to our hand, in the absence of better modes, and to accept what commerce will, with or without our artistic leave, be sure to take, on account of lowness of cost and rapidity of application. I mean that the absolute permanence of the dye for most of the purposes for which Tusser silk will be used is of less importance than the development and utilisation of so eminently useful a product of nature.

There are plenty of permanent dyes at hand for Tusser silk for embroidery and artistic purposes if artists will only be content to use those natural colours which the best dyes will yield to this silk, and not require combination and tones which are unsuitable both to these dyes and to this silk. Such colours are darkish shades of subdued blue, gold, yellow, low-toned purples, strong reds, greens, &c.

Amongst the numerous dye-stuffs indigenous to India or which I have received samples for examination, by order of Her Majesty's Government of India, I may mention the following as being the best adapted for dyeing Tusser silk; and others will, no doubt, appear as my examination proceeds:—

Lac.
Safflower.
Leaves of Phyllanthus emblica.
Calyces of Thespesia populnea.
Flowers of Butea frondosa.
Indigo.
Hursinghar flowers (especially good).
Flowers of Cedrela toona (very good).

In addition to the above, I may mention the following as being useful dyes, though not yielding such rich colours as those previously mentioned :—

Mùnjeet (root of *Rubia munjista*).
Cotton flowers.
Sapan wood.
Flowers of Grislea tomentosa.
Root of Morinda citrifolia.
Ashna bark.
Root bark of Ventilago maderaspatana

The following also, although the colours produced by them are poor in comparison to the preceding, will be found to yield useful results with Tusser silk :—

Seeds of Cassia tora.
Pista phul.
Bark of Euphorbia tirucalli.
Pomegranate rind.

That Tusser silk should be more difficult to dye than mulberry silk may well be inferred from the difference in degree of solubility of the two silks. A neutral solution of chloride of zinc gently heated dissolves mulberry silk instantly, whilst it only dissolves Tusser silk slowly. In a cold solution I found it took three days to dissolve mulberry silk, but with Tusser silk a fortnight's immersion produced no effect.

Similar effects are also produced by an ammoniacal solution of copper oxide, which has the property of effecting the solution of both silks in the cold more quickly. The cold solution rapidly dissolves mulberry silk and also cotton. It dissolves Tusser silk more slowly, but its effect on wool is simply to blacken it without dissolving it.

As the preparation of this solution requires care, it may be well if I explain the method :—

1. Make a strong aqueous solution of sulphate of copper.
2. When cold, add to this solution a few drops of strong ammonia until the whitish-blue colour formed begins to change to a deeper blue.

3. This whitish-blue colour is due to formation of a precipitate, which wash several times with water on a filter.
4. Dissolve the precipitate in cold concentrated ammonia.

CHAPTER VII.

Tusser Embroidery.

Tusser silk, being lustrous and strong, is peculiarly suitable for embroidery when reeled from the cocoon and manufactured into floss. This new use of it has been found by Mrs. Wardle, who by the employment of suitably dyed shades has succeeded in obtaining very excellent effects on a ground Tusser silk cloth, specimens of which are in the collection, Nos. 50 and 52, lent by the Royal School of Art Needlework, and No. 47, lent and coloured by Mrs. Wardle, and worked by herself and the Leek School of Embroidery. The old Indian print designs look remarkably well in some of her colour combinations, as in the antimacassars represented in Plate LV. and Nos. 50 and 52 in the Museum collection. In every instance the use of violent or crude shades has been avoided, and the effects are singularly soft and pleasing.

It can be also used in combination with mulberry-worm silk on grounds of other material, and also to heighten up the effects of crewel wool work, as well as in a variety of other ways which will readily suggest themselves to embroidery workers.

A good way is to print on the cloth designs of established worth, and to embroider the designs so printed. (*See* Plate LV.)

Another way is that in which the Japanese are so exceedingly clever, to have a design worked out partly with embroidery and partly in print colours. The effect is excellent.

The effects may be varied *ad infinitum*, and I commend this mode as a valuable addition to the embroideress's art. There is for it a mixed result, avoiding a monotony of effect one so often sees in modern embroidery, and also less monotony for the worker as well as a large scope for her interest and skill.

Further information of the new embroidery will be found in a very interesting little manual recently issued, entitled

"Handbook of Embroidery," written by Miss Higgin, and edited by Lady Marian Alford, and published and sold by the Royal School of Art Needlework, South Kensington.

CHAPTER VIII.

THE ERIA SILKWORM.

The *Eria* silkworm, or *Attacus ricini*, feeds on the *Palma Christi*, or castor-oil plant, *Ricinis communis*.

It is a native of Assam, and according to Mr. Geoghegan is found to the south-west in a track comprising the districts of Nepaul, Kumaon, Ladak, Darjeeling Dinagepore, Rungpore, and perhaps parts of Bhangulpore and Purmiah, and in Assam (*see* map, Plate XXV.) In 1791 Sir W. Jones drew attention to this silk, and Dr. Roxburgh in 1804. In Assam the worm spins a white silk, whilst in Dinagepore the colour of the cocoon is brown.

Dr. A. Wallace states that there are two kinds of caterpillars, one white and the other green, the white caterpillars invariably spinning red silk and the green ones white.

The leaves of the castor-oil plant, *Ricinis communis* or *Palma Christi*, are the best and commonest food, but it will also feed on the following:—

Koosool.
Hindograss.
Murkurdal.
Okonnee.
Gomaree.
Litta Pakoree.
Birzonally.
Xanthoxylon hostile.
Coriaria nipalensis.
Ailanthus glandulosa.
Ailanthus excelsa.

Probably the most complete account of the *Attacus ricini* is by Mr. Geoghegan, in his report on the Silk Industry of India, of which I avail myself to gather some useful particulars.

The *Attacus ricini*, according to Dr. Buchanan, feeds both on *Ricinus communis* and *Ricinus viridis*.

The female moth lays her eggs round a twig and then dies. These twigs are sold in the markets covered with eggs, the dead moths frequently hanging to them, and presenting a very curious appearance.

The caterpillar moults four times, and when fully grown is about 3½ inches long.

According to Mr. Hugon, the natives soften the cocoon in potash, and draw the silk off roughly with the finger and thumb, thus making a kind of spun silk. Dr. Buchanan, however, says the silk is also wound on a reel in Dinagepore.

M. Guérin Méneville stated, in 1860, that it was impossible to reel this cocoon. I am certainly disposed to think it is quite impracticable to reel it. Still there is a method of using at hand, and I know of no silk better adapted for spinning.

Dr. Helfer, in 1837, states in the Journal of the Asiatic Society in Bengal, that this worm is so productive as to give sometimes twelve broods of silk in the year, and that it grows rapidly, and offers no difficulty whatever for an extensive speculation.

Mr. Geoghegan says, with regard to the thread from cocoons of *Attacus ricini*, that a seer of 96 sicca weight ($2\frac{464}{1000}$ lbs.) of this thread is worth from annas 12 (one shilling and sixpence) to R. 1 (two shillings); but it is very seldom sold, and the people who keep the insect rear no more than is just sufficient to make clothes for their own families.

Mr. Michael Atkinson, of Singapore, describes the cloth made of Eria to be of incredible durability, the life of one person being seldom sufficient to wear out a garment made of it, so that the same piece descends from mother to daughter.

The thickness of this fibre is $\frac{1}{1500}$ of an inch on the outside of the cocoon, and $\frac{1}{1450}$ in the inner part. For other particulars see table on page 68.

Mr. Hugon says that, "in Assam, the quantity of Eria " cloth the merchants used to take away was very con- " siderable, but in the latter years of the Assam Rajah's " rule, from the disorganised state of the country, the " number of merchants gradually diminished. The quantity " the country is capable of exporting under an improved " management would be very large, for it forms at present " the dress of the poorer classes at all seasons, and is used " by the highest for winter wear.

"So long ago as 1769 vast quantities were being produced in the country around Guraghaut." He estimated the annual production at 1,000 maunds, or 82,000 lbs. "In the " district of Dunung the annual yield of Eria is 1,000

" maunds, of which one third is exported either in the " form of cocoons or woven into heavy cloths (Borkapor.)"

Mr. Hugon stated, that for want of a proper solvent of the gum the natives could not reel the cocoons. I am disposed to believe the reason to be in the soft and irregular way the worm excretes the silk. It forms its cocoon much more loosely than the mulberry worm, and not being cemented like the Tusser cocoon it becomes ravelled in the attempt to reel it. Mr. Brownlow states that in Cachar the *Eria* or *Ricini* worm is trained by the Cacharis, a people living in isolated villages on the hills. They soften the cocoons in a mixture of cowdung and water, and they are then carried off to a spindle by the women of the tribe. This silk is dyed by the natives with lac, munjeet, and indigo; but owing to its being much inferior to the silk of commerce in taking dyes, only very poor colours are obtained, the process for dyeing being too rude and unscientific. But there is a good use for it, and that is by the same means I have pointed out for Tusser and other wild silks of India; namely, for spinning instead of reeling.

The natives of India use Eria silk for the manufacture of garments, having the following names:—

Borkapor.
Meklas (petticoats).
Rhiha (scarves).
Goursha.

At page 58 will be found an account of the important results I have obtained by spinning and weaving the silk of this worm.

The *Eria* or *Attacus ricini* must not be confounded with the *Attacus cynthia* or *Ailanthus* worm domesticated to a small extent in Europe. The cocoons of the two are essentially different (*see* Plate XVIII., Fig. 3, and Plate XX., Fig. 2). I mention this because of the lengthened efforts in France and elsewhere to make the *Ailanthus*-fed silk available to commerce. It has not yet found its way into the market to any but a tentative and experimental extent.

Attacus cynthia comes originally from China, and feeds on the *Ailanthus glandulosa.* Its cocoons were first received in Europe in November 1856, and hatched out the following year, and towards the middle of May 1857 the first living specimen of *Attacus cynthia* was born in Europe. These cocoons were sent by Abbé Fantoni, a Piedmontese missionary, from the province of Shan Tung, in the north of China, situate just south of Pekin, to some friends at Turin. This species was first introduced into England in 1859, and reared by Mr. F. Moore, of the East India Museum. The larvæ, feeding on the *castor-oil* plant and hatched from eggs sent by M. Guérin Méneville, were exhibited by Mr. Moore, before the Entomological Society of London, in October 1859. Afterwards Lady Dorothy Nevill cultivated the species extensively in this country.* Plates VIII., XVIII., XIX., XX., illustrate the entomological characteristics of *Attacus cynthia* and *Attacus ricini*.

In a despatch to the Right Honourable the Marquis of Hartington, Her Majesty's Secretary of State for India, dated Simla, the 1st of June 1880, and signed by Lord Lytton, late Viceroy of India; Sir F. P. Haines, G.C.B., G.C.S.I.; Sir John Strachey, G.C.S.I.; Gen. Sir Edwin B. Johnson, K.C.B., C.I.E.; A. Rivers Thompson, C.S.I.; and Maj.-Gen. A. Fraser, R.E., the following statements occur:—

"In Bengal, small supplies of the (Eria) silk are at present worked up chiefly for home manufacture and use; but there is no reason to suppose that production would not be stimulated if remunerative prices could be obtained.

"In Assam, it will be observed that in only a few of the northern districts and in the Jaintia Hills can the silk (Eria) be procured at present in any appreciable quantities. From these districts it is estimated that 84,000 lbs. of raw silk could be obtained annually. Elsewhere a very limited amount of the silk is produced, not as an article of external trade, but for home consumption. But as the necessary food for the *Eria* silkworm grows in abundance in Assam, it seems probable, as suggested by the Chief Commissioner, that an effective demand would lead to a large increase of production."

A letter to the Secretary to the Government of India accompanying the above despatch, dated Calcutta 26th April 1880, and signed by Babu Rajendra Nath Mitra, states as follows:—

"The districts in which Eria silk can be obtained are Rungpore, Dinagepore, Bogra, Julpigoree, Darjeeling, Chittagong, Gya, Shahabad, Purneah, and Pooree.

"In the Bogra and Julpigoree districts the silk is not worked up as an article of trade, but for home consumption only; about 18 maunds of cocoons being annually produced in Bogra, and about 40 to 50 maunds of thread in Julpigoree. In Darjeeling about 10 to 12 maunds of cocoons could be annually obtained in the Terai.

* Dr. Wallace on Ailanthiculture. See "Transactions of the Entomological Society for 1866."

"In the Chittagong district the silk is worked to a very limited extent, the insects being tied on plum trees from which the cocoons are gathered. The thread is made into twine for fishing purposes, and is considered strong and lasting. About Rs. 300 worth of this twine is sold annually in the local bazaars.

"In Gya the silk is worked to a small extent in certain wild tracts of that district, while in Shahabad the quantity produced during the year amounts to about 9,000 lbs.

"In Pooree the *Eria* worm can be seen on castor-oil plants, and is believed to be common, though entirely neglected by the natives. The worm is reported to be very common on the Government estate of Khoorda, where the plant on which it feeds, the '*nalbeli,*' said to belong to the moonseed order, grows in abundance."

The following particulars are derived from a letter, also accompanying the previously mentioned despatch, to the Collector of Poonah, from W. C. Taylor, Esq., Settlement Officer, Khoorda, dated Khoorda, 30th December 1879 :—

"I forward some specimens of an *Attacus* found very plentifully in the Khoorda jungles.

"The caterpillars feed on a very common plant called the *Nalbeli,* the botanical name of which I have not been able to ascertain, but Dr. Stewart thinks it belongs to the moonseed order.

"The worm may be called a monthly worm, as there are many broods in the year, and I have now a brood of worms which are just spinning ; the cold weather has, however, delayed their coming to maturity very much.

"This species is very hardy and easy to rear, either in confinement or in the open ; and as they produce so many crops of good silk in the year, and there is such an abundant supply of food, I am sure it would pay well to encourage production of this silk in Khoorda, and I can, if desired, procure a bale of 50 lbs. of the cocoons.

"The inhabitants of Khoorda appear to be quite ignorant of the value of the silk, and, so far as I can ascertain, the cocoons have never before been collected on the estate.

"Even the Tusser cocoons are not collected to any extent, and the cultivation of Tusser is not known in Khoorda, although the value of Tusser is known, and there are reelers and weavers of the silk on the estate."

The following are extracts from a letter, which also accompanies the foregoing despatch, to the Officiating Secretary to the Government of India Home, Revenue, and Agricultural Department, from S. O. B. Ridsdale, Esq., C.S.,

Secretary to the Chief Commissioner of Assam, dated Shillong, the 20th September 1879 :—

"At present about 54,000 lbs. of Eria silk in the raw state, unreeled, can be obtained annually from the districts of Kamrup, Darrang Nowgong, and Lakhimpur, and about 30,000 lbs. from the Jaintia Hills. In the districts of Goalpara and Sibsagar the production of silk is carried on to a very limited extent, chiefly for home consumption. In Cachar it is not an article of trade, but the silk is worked up by the hill tribes in almost every village of the North Cachar Hills for their own use. The Deputy Commissioner of Sylhet reports that he cannot learn of any of this silk being produced in his district. But here, as well as throughout the whole of this province, the necessary food for the *Eria* silkworm grows in profuse abundance, and there seems no reason to doubt that, if the people of this province could be induced to turn their attention to the production of this silk, an almost unlimited supply could be obtained."

The "Times Weekly Edition," of July 2nd 1880, makes the following statement :—

"An attempt is being made to establish a silk-producing industry in the Dehra Doon district, in the North-West Provinces, and in Gurdaspore district, in the Punjab. The experiments are under the management of Mr. Lepper, agent for Messrs. Lister and Co. of Bradford. Mr. Lepper has offered handsome prizes to the ryots growing the best mulberry and castor-oil plant (this latter, no doubt, for Eria sericulture plantations), and producing the best out-turn of silk. There seems to be good reason to hope that the experiment may succeed, and a new and prosperous industry be set on foot in Upper India."

CHAPTER IX.

Dyeing of Eria Silk.

The dyeing of Eria silk much resembles the dyeing of Tusser. Whether owing to the flatness of its fibre, or to the nature of its sericine, it is far behind mulberry silk in its natural affinity for dyestuffs. Heat and the media of mineral salts, however, are the principal agents in bringing the fibre into a dye-receiving subjection. The specimen skeins of dyed Eria silk, Nos. 60 and 61 in the Collection, are favourable examples of what I have been able to effect in dyeing this silk. The dyeing baths have to be much stronger in tinctorial matter than those for mulberry silks. It follows, therefore, that there is an unavoidable increase in the cost of dyeing Eria silk, as is also the case in Tusser silk, and to about the same extent. Probably I shall not be far from accuracy in stating that Eria silk requires twice as much dyestuff as mulberry silk, thereby causing the dyeing to cost considerably more. The Eria cocoons being of two kinds, some of them rust colour and others white, cannot be dyed into pale colours without bleaching, which again adds to the cost of dyeing. It bleaches very well with the bioxide of barium process, and takes excellent colours in pale tints afterwards. For dark shades bleaching is not necessary, nor would it be necessary for paler shades in silk spun from the white cocoons if they could be kept separate from the brown ones.

From the specimens in the Collection it will be seen that I have succeeded in imparting a variety of colours to this silk which leave little or nothing to be desired. As far as I can learn, I believe this is the first time in Europe that Eria silk has been dyed. If it has been attempted, certainly no such colours have been obtained as those in the Collection.

The geographical distribution of Tusser silk is one of the most important and promising features in the present effort to extend its utilities. It is found almost, if not entirely, over the whole of India as well as in British Burma; the cocoons are everywhere. It has a larger area of growth by far than cotton, and probably may be produced as extensively. That a great future is in store for it is certain. Labour is cheap in India, and the natives cannot too soon turn their attention to rearing the worms and collecting and reeling the silk for exportation to Europe.

No one can doubt that when it is found that any fibre can be utilised extensively, and that fibre has a wider range than cotton, the chances of an abundant supply under cultivation are almost certainties, and it is then only a question of time and perseverence to bring it into the market at prices which will cause it to be sought after and used as extensively as it deserves.

This argument has been well used by Mr. T. Dickins, Chairman of the Silk Supply Association, with reference to the mulberry-fed silkworm of commerce; for wherever the mulberry tree will grow and come into leaf at the same time as the eggs of *Bombyx mori* are hatched, there can silk be cultivated. This also gives for mulberry silk a wider range of growth than cotton, and probably before long several of our Ultra-Austral colonies may begin to export silk. The cost of colonial labour seems to be the only hindrance.

In a correspondence I had with Mr. Lister since this report appeared he informed me that Eria and Muga silk are, to his mind far before Tusser; but any of them could be used profitably when all the conditions of profitable success are duly considered. He feels no manner of doubt that, with time and patience, wild silks will be profitably used. With regard to Tusser, he says that when it is reeled by the natives it is so full of faults as to be dear at any price, and when reeled by Europeans so costly as not to pay. This adds another strong argument in favour of my earnest recommendation to the Government of India that the natives of India, whose time is less valuable and labour less costly, should be taught the European methods of reeling. He asks, "As to Eria, is it simply a question of cost of production in the first place, and then can it be reeled? If not, can it be produced so cheaply as to pay to use it for combing and spinning?" My reply is emphatically, "Abandon all ideas of reeling Eria silk; the cocoon is too soft, and the fibres mingled together too irregularly, to afford any hope of successful reeling commercially. Produce it on a large scale, comb and spin it, and the success is complete." Mr. Lister's opinions are of the highest possible value, as he is probably the largest spun-silk manufacturer in Europe, and, besides his immense spinning establishment at Manningham near Bradford, he has sent out to India a large and expensive staff to cultivate the wild silks and the plants on which the worms feed, and has gone there himself in order that the experiments may be carried out under his own supervision.

CHAPTER X.

The Moonga, Mooga, or Muga Silk.

This silk is produced from the worm known as the *Moonga*, *Muga*, or *Mooga*, *Antheræa Assama* (Helfer); also the *Saturnia Assama* of Westwood. It is found in Assam, and also sparingly in the Dehra Doon, and is the next in importance to Tusser (*see* Map, Plate XXVI.) Mr. Geoghegan's description of this silk occupies three pages of the Blue-book on the Silk Industry of India, from which I abstract the following particulars:—

"The worm that gives the common fawn-coloured Moonga silk when fed on the most common plants gives a whitish silk when fed on the leaves on which other worms feed. The plants it feeds on are named and estimated as follows:—

"No. 1. *Champa* (*Michelia champaca*).—The silk produced from the worm feeding on this plant gives the finest and whitest silk, used only by the rajah and great people, and is called *champa pattea Moonga*. The thread is sold at from 11 to 12 rupees a seer (11*s.* to 12*s.* per lb.)

"No. 2. *Maizankurra* (called also *addakurry*). The old trees are cut down and the jungle about burnt, and the worms are fed upon the tender leaves of the off-shoots for one year, when the leaves become too old and hard for the worms. Silk is sold at 6 to 7 rupees per seer (6*s.* to 7*s.* per lb.).

"No. 3. *Soom* (*Sarcostemma brevistigma*).—This is the common tree of the vicinity; the silk from the worms fed on this gives the finest sort of fawn-coloured Moonga. Silk is sold at 3½ to 4 rupees per seer (3*s.* 6*d.* to 4*s.* per lb.)

"No. 4. *Soonhalloo* (*Tetranthera macrophylla*).—This is also a brown silk of inferior quality. This plant is most common in Dhurumpore and about Russa Chokey.

"No. 5. *Digluttee* (*Tetranthera doglottica*).—This is also brown silk of inferior quality, but the worms fed on the leaves of this tree increase much in size.

"No. 6. *Pattees hoonda* (*Laurus obtusifolia*).

"The worm also feeds on the *Kontooloa*.

"The Monga worm gives broods five times a year, and the cocoon is very large, but thin. I could only obtain silk the produce of worms feeding on Nos. 3 and 4, and manufactured into cheap cloths for the lower classes.

"In its natural fawn colour it stands washing much better than ordinary silk, keeping gloss and colour till the last."*

Mr. Geoghegan, on page 114 of his "Silk Industry of India," says:—

The cycle of the insect is thus given:—

From emergence from the egg to commencement of cocoon	-	30 days.
In the cocoon	-	20 ,,
As a moth	-	6 ,,
In the egg	-	10 ,,
Total	-	66 days.

There are five broods per year.

* Geoghegan, "Silk Industry of India," p. 25.

In 1873 Colonel Hopkinson, the Commissioner of Assam gave more modern figures :—

"It thence appears that the Soom forests (on which the worm is chiefly fed) cover an area of about 34,000 acres, of which about 18,000 are assessed, yielding a revenue of nearly Rs. 28,000 (2,800*l*.). By far the greater portion of the assessed area lies in the district of Sibsagar. The production of the silk is said to employ some 48,000 persons, but it is not their sole calling. The out-turn of silk is estimated at upwards of 100,000 lbs. But as it is admitted that the greater part of the silk is reserved for home manufacture, this estimate cannot be regarded as absolutely trustworthy. The price of the yarn per seer (2 lbs.) varies from Rs. 5 (10*s*.) to Rs. 9 (18*s*.) in the several districts. The small portion exported goes to Calcutta and Dacca. From the former place it is said to find its way to some extent to Bhangulpur and Bombay.

"The Silk Committee of the Nigri Horticultural Society reported favourably on some Munga silk sent down by Captain Jenkins in 1839, and expressed their opinion that the article was calculated to become of extensive and valuable use to our home manufacturers."*

One acre of land yields 50,000 Muga-silk cocoons, which yield upwards of 12 seers (24 lbs.) of silk, price Rs. 5 per seer, or 5*s*. per lb.

From Mr. Hugon's description of the mode of reeling it is evident it is of the rudest kind, and points to a remedy in the improved continental reeling appliances.

The following particulars by Mr. Hugon in 1834 are interesting :—The Muga silk industry is confined to Assam and some Tipperat villages. The quantity of land planted with food for the Muga was 5,000 acres, capable of yielding 1,500 maunds (123,000 lbs.), of silk. This silk formed one of the principal exports of Assam. The average quantity was 257 maunds (21,070 lbs.), valued at Rs. 56,054 (5,605*l*.), leaving the country principally in the shape of thread. He advocates the use of the Moonga silk in coloured fabrics, it being easily dyed.

The diameter of the fibres of Muga silk taken from the external part of the cocoon averages $\frac{1}{1430}$ inch, but the external fibres are very variable. The diameter of the inner and less variable fibres is $\frac{1}{1080}$ inch. The outer fibres will break with a weight of $2\frac{1}{8}$ drams on the average, but the inner will support three drams. The tension of the

---

* Geoghegan, "Silk Industry of India," p. 25.

outer fibres averages one inch to the foot, and of the inner $1\frac{3}{4}$ inches. All the fibres are, like Tusser, flat and striated, and united by the gum in pairs by their edges.

The following table is given by Mr. Hugon, showing the nature and prices of the various kinds of cloth made from Moonga silk:—

Name of Cloth.	Size of Yards and Inches.	Weights.		Price of Thread.		Cost of Weaving.		Total.		Remarks.
		lbs.	*oz.*	*s.*	*d.*	*s.*	*d.*	*s.*	*d.*	
Goovias - - -	4×30 in.		12	3	9		$4\frac{1}{2}$	4	$1\frac{1}{2}$	Dhoties.
Ditto - - -	9×1–4 in.	2	0	10	0	1	0	11	0	(Dhoties.)
Mekla - - -	$2\frac{3}{4}$×1		8	2	6		3	2	9	Petticoats.
Rhia - -	$6\frac{3}{4}$× $\frac{3}{4}$	1	0	5	0		6	5	6	Scarfs.
Gaursha - - -	$4\frac{1}{2}$×20 in.		4	1	3		$1\frac{1}{2}$	1	$4\frac{1}{2}$	Worn as turbans or round the waist.
Poonta Boor Cappor -	$6\frac{3}{4}$×$1\frac{1}{4}$	2	0	4	0		9	4	9	Made of the floss and worn in winter.

Plates V. and VI. illustrate the entomology of this species.

CHAPTER XI.

Carding and Spinning Eria and Muga Cocoons.

In consequence of a suggestion I made to the Government of India in 1879, instructions were sent out to the Eria and Muga districts for the collection of a quantity of both kinds of cocoons, and in November and December 1879 I received five cases containing 70 lbs. of Eria cocoons and 45 lbs. of Muga cocoons.

These I at once sent to my spinners with instructions to them to card or dress and spin the cocoons and return the silk to me with samples showing each stage of the process, particularly in yarns, for weaving, knitting, sewing, and embroidery purposes, and in woven fabrics.

The cocoons were subjected by them to a thoroughly exhaustive treatment, and I have very great pleasure in describing the results of the operations, which happily have been most successful.

Specimens of the silk at the end of every operation were sent to me which exemplified the result of each process. The staples carded from the cocoons were most beautiful and valuable, and the yarns and cloths resolved from these staples were of such a character that I feel sure it can only be a question of a short time to develop the carding, spinning, and weaving of these silks into a most useful and extensive industry, if it is possible in India to have a co-extensive production of Eria and Muga worms.

In the case of the Eria the staple obtained from the first draft's operation is glossy, long, and very fine. (*See* specimen, 1st draft, No. 58, in the Collection at the Indian Museum.) Its fineness is owing to that of the ultimate fibre. It is about one half finer than Tusser silk, although not more than two thirds as fine as the Bengal mulberry-fed silk of *Bombyx mori*, or silk of commerce. The after or shorter drafts are also of much importance as showing the economising of the shorter fibres after the longer ones have been removed. These are used for less important manufactures than the long staple. Nothing is wasted in the modern mode of spinning. The yarns made of these fibres are of great regularity and fineness, proving this silk capable of uses for spinning and weaving purposes to an unlimited extent.

It would not be worth while to waste time in encouraging efforts to wind or reel the Eria cocoon. Its proper and simple destination is the carding frame, and from thence to be spun. This is the only way to develop it into an extensive industry, and one for which, on account of the modern spinning machinery, a large demand is already waiting.

Woven cloths of great strength and durability can be made from yarns spun from Eria silk, and these cloths appear to take printing matter very well. (*See* the undyed fabrics woven in a variety of designs, Nos. 64, 65, and 66 in the Museum collection.)

The staple produced from the Muga cocoon is excellent. The silk appears to be naturally of a much darker colour than Eria, but I am not sure if this is not owing to circumstances that may be controlled.

The woven specimen comes out of the loom very much darker than I anticipated, and does not bleach so well as Eria. It promises, however, to be a most useful and valuable silk, if it can be obtained or cultivated in quantity. Any quantity, however large, would be easily bought up for spinning. Mr. Blair, of Glasgow, informs me that he has sent out to Assam for a ton of Muga cocoons for experimental purposes. I think it will prove to take dyes more freely than the Eria, and is well worth investigation.

I feel certain, from the comparative fineness of the fibre, that this silk is undeveloped both as a reeled and thrown product, and that organzine and tram of finer deniers than Tusser could be obtained from the cocoons as well as a regular and even thread. The cocoon is larger and firmer than that of the Eria, and can be reeled without difficulty.

My spinners have suggested that the Government of India should authorise the collection of a few hundred pounds more of Muga cocoons for further developements; and in supporting their suggestion, I hope, for the purpose of seeing what can be done in dyeing and printing this silk, that the Government of India may consent to send for the necessary quantity. My spinners would, if requested, buy the whole or part of them, and have requested me to urge the collection of wild silks in India, so that much greater quantities may be put in the market, the demand in England, France, and Germany being already enormous.

The following is a copy of a letter from Messrs. Clayton, Marsdens, and Co., who are the largest silk spinners in Halifax, and well illustrates the large demand which exists at present for wild silks:—

"The manipulation of the waste products of Tusser and other wild silks has been a study with my firm for some years past, and we have arrived at such a state of perfection in the yarns produced from them that we may fairly say that as an industry it is thoroughly established.

"These waste products consist of the foul and spoilt threads thrown off in the process of reeling from the cocoon, of the husks remaining when the reeling is completed, of spoilt or pierced cocoons, and of the waste made in winding the reeled silk for manufacturing purposes. All these products are now of value, and the demand for them is largely on the increase, consequent upon the extended demand for the improved yarns now made from them. They have been found particularly suitable for silk plushes, a trade largely on the increase for shawls and other garments, and for the manufacture of dress materials. The demand for these yarns for some of the above purposes, at present, far exceeds the supply. In the face of these facts, the supply of the raw material becomes a most important question, and the efforts of the Government of India to develop the resources of India to meet this increasing demand are very timely, and must prove beneficial both to the natives of our Indian Empire and to many manufacturing industries at home.

"The silk from the specimens of Eria and Muga cocoons worked by my firm is of a most brilliant and rich character, as will be seen from the specimens now exhibited in the Indian section of the South Kensington Museum. Their spinning qualities are quite equal to any of the wild silks from China.

"What is required is to encourage the natives to collect these waste silks and develop facilities for bringing them to market, and here I may make a few guiding remarks as to the collecting and packing of these products.

"I may say that waste silk in any form is of value, more especially the large cocoons of the Muga and Eria species. But it should be well understood that, for *use as waste silk, no cocoons should be sent to this country with the chrysalis or worm in them.* It will be obvious why, when it is stated that the worm or the dust of the worm in the cocoon is of no value whatever, and that the weight of these worms many times exceeds the weight of silk in each cocoon.

"Pierced cocoons, or cocoons out of which the worm has worked itself, are the most valuable as waste for spinning purposes. But all the classes named above are suitable, and may be collected and forwarded with profit to this country.

"In collecting and packing these, it is of importance to avoid admixture with any foreign or vegetable matter in the shape of sticks, straw, and dirt, as much as possible. The cleaner the shipments are, the better the prices they will command in our market."

Muga silk is much better to dye than either Tusser or Eria; it takes both the aniline and older dyes very freely, and better colour can be more easily obtained than upon Tusser or Eria silk, and at less cost. I have dyed some beautiful colours upon Muga yarns which came from India, for the Paris Exhibition.

CHAPTER XII.

Attacus Atlas.

The next species I will describe is the *Attacus Atlas* of Linnæus, which is also known by the following names:—

Phalæna Attacus Atlas (Linn.)
Bombyx Atlas (Fabricius).
Saturnia Silhetica (Helfer).

The imago or perfect moth of this species is the largest of all the silk moths. As will be seen by Plates IX. and X., it is a grand insect. It is called in France, *Le Géant des Papillons.* The largest specimens measure upwards of 10 in. in expanse of wing. According to Horsfield it feeds on the *Melokko* (*Phyllanthus emblica*), a plant known also in India as *Kupu gaga.* Mr. Geoghegan says the silkworm is found in Mussoorce on the *Falconeria insignia, Bradleia ovata,* and other plants ; in Kumaon, on the *barberry,* where it is abundant, and also eastward to Cachar.

A letter dated Khoorda, 30th December 1879, from W. C. Taylor, Esq., which I have previously mentioned in speaking of the *Eria* worm, states that *Attacus Atlas* is found in Khoorda, and, like the *Eria* worm, feeds on the "*Nalbeli,*" which Dr. Stewart supposes to belong to the *Moonseed* order. It feeds, too, on the *Soom* tree, *Sarcostemma brevistigma.* Mr. P. H. Gosse has written a most interesting life-history of this species, describing all that is known of it. His paper, from which I quote a few pertinent facts, will be found in the "Entomologist" of February and March 1879. He says, "It is a widespread species ranging over the South and East half of Asia, continental and insular, common on the slopes of the Himalaya, and all through India to the points of both peninsulas; abundant in China; scattered over the isles of the Archipelago, from Java to the Moluccas, to Borneo and the Philippines, a range of 35° of latitude and 55° of longitude."

His efforts to breed the *Atlas* worm in England are described; and although he has not been very successful, owing to sickness and death in the larval stage, his account is very interesting. Captain Landy, of Surbiton, has succeeded in obtaining fifteen good cocoons from twenty-four eggs, the larvæ having been fed on the common *barberry.* Mr. Gosse has fed his on the *sallow,* others on the plum and apple tree leaves. He states that all the family of *Saturniidæ* are very polyphagous.

It is interesting to observe the micaceous or window-like spot on each of the four wings. These, although characteristic of the *Saturniidæ,* are almost more largely developed in *Attacus Atlas* than in any other species. The French call these vitreous membranes *porte-miroirs.*

There are several varieties of *Attacus Atlas* which show their divergence from the type by the variations of these fusiform window-like ornamentations. In some they are single, in others double.

The diameter of the external fibres of the cocoon is very variable, averaging about $\frac{1}{1820}$ inch, whilst that of the internal fibres is more uniform, and about $\frac{1}{1000}$ inch. The outer fibres are capable of supporting an average weight of $2\frac{1}{8}$ drams, and the inner $2\frac{1}{2}$ drams. The tension of the outer fibres is one inch to the foot, and the inner $1\frac{1}{4}$ inches. The fibres are flat and longitudinally striated, and united in pairs by their edges.

The egg of *Attacus Atlas* is $\frac{8}{100}$ of a inch long. The larvæ moult six times. The cocoon of *Attacus Atlas* is from two to three inches long, and about one inch wide at the widest part, and weighs two grammes, or the $\frac{1}{14}$th of an ounce.

Mr. Gosse says, "The colour of the cocoon is a light umber, or drab; its surface (independently of the impress of leaves) roughly granular, scarcely at all silky or floccose, except at the mouth; its substance thin, parchmenty, very firm; the interior very smooth, and even sub-glossy. The upper extremity forms a natural orifice for the exit of the moth, made by the conveyance of a great number of silk-fibres, which are left ungummed, and are thus soft and flossy, the gummed, stiff silk passing up on one side and contracting into the cord. Thus the cocoon is not closed, like those of *Bombyx mori*, of *Telea*, of the *Antheræa*, but open, like those of *A. cynthia*, of the *Samiæ*, of the *Saturniæ*. As a result of this structure, the exit of the imago leaves no disturbance behind, no witness, no disarrangement of these soft fibres, such as is the case with Yama-mai, Pernyi, and Mylitta (*Antheræa mylitta*)."

Mr. Geoghegan states the silk to be difficult to reel, though it reels partially if boiled with vinegar. Captain Hutton says the silk is decidedly good, and Dr. Chavannes, of Lausanne, considers its introduction into France desirable. He says the worm is the *Fagara* of China, where it has long been cultivated.

A Government Report gives the following particulars with regard to the food plants of the *Attacus Atlas*:—

1. *Phakeera* (*Cinchonaceæ*).

2. New name, probably a laurel, foliage redolent of prussic acid, fruit like a plum kernel, containing a large portion of oil resembling that of bitter almonds, stature large; not very common.

3. A tree resembling the China tea plant, of frequent

occurrence as a weed in tea gardens; stature middling; common in jhum lands, less so in primitive forests.

4. *Nagdana* (*Artimisia sp.*).

5. *Monphul* (Cachar name), known in Dacca as the *Myna kata.*

6. *Balos*, a weed fed on also by the *Attacus Canningi.*

7. *Koorkooree*, one of the commonest of *jhum* weeds, one of the most eligible for training the *Atlas* worm.

8. *Lutki* (*Osbeckia*), a very small plant, but the silk off it is very white.

9. *Bon Chelita*, a large, hardy, rapidly growing tree, sufficiently common for the purposes of silk cultivation.

10. *Kadam* (*Nauclea*).

11. *Chelita* (*Dellenia speciosa*), eminently adapted for training the *Atlas* worm.

12. *Boidraj* (*Padrelace ?*) The silk off this plant is very dark.

13. *Lood*, also fed on by *Attacus Canningi.*

CHAPTER XIII.

Various other Wild Silk-Producing Worms.

Antheræa yama-mai.

This species is a native of Japan, although it is found also in China, and has been introduced into India, thougn very sparingly.

In Japan its silk is said to be most highly prized, and reserved for the use of Royalty; but as to being so of late years I am inclined to doubt, as the silk is not very fine, and I saw many woven specimens of it in the Japanese silk exhibits in the Paris Exhibition of 1878. The cocoon is of a beautiful pale-green colour (Plate XVIII., Fig. 2). It has been naturalised in Europe, and is a very hardy species.

A cross between the *A. yama-mai* and *Bombyx Attacus pernyi* is a great success in France. It is so hardy that hatching is said to take place at freezing-point. I have recommended the Government of India to encourage the acclimatisation of this species in India, as I feel certain it yields a most useful species of silk; and although a coarser fibre than that of *Bombyx mori*, it is finer than that of *Antheræa paphia*, and it has a very glossy appearance being flat and striated. The diameter of the fibres is $\frac{1}{1000}$ of an inch. Owing to the want of sufficient quantity I have not been able to test its dyeing capabilities, but I have no doubt it can be dyed with moderate facility in all colours, though it may not yield as complete a whiteness as China silk. The Japanese had some very interesting fabrics of this silk in the Paris Exhibition of 1878. Some were composed of *A. yama-mai* silk entirely, and some of *Bombyx mori* silk ornamented with stripes of *A. yama-mai* undyed, giving a pleasing variety with its greenish-white appearance.

Samples of fibres and fabrics made of *yama-mai* silk will be found, Nos. 81 and 82, in the collection. The entomology of the species is illustrated in Plates XVII. and XVIII.

The following is extracted from "Cassell's Technical Educator," and is the translation of a notice published by M. Pompe van Meedervoort relative to the introduction of the *Yama-mai* into Europe:—

"In 1862 I had the honour to make the aquaintance of M. Eugène Simon. He informed me of the great value of the *Bombyx Yama-mai*, and together we made every effort, but in vain, to procure eggs of this species; we were told it was absolutely impossible to obtain them. M. Simon being obliged to return, I made him promise before he left to continue my efforts, and in case of success to offer the eggs to the French Government. But the more I tried, the more I saw how difficult, if not impossible, was the attempt. I applied in vain to the Japanese merchants, the silk growers, to many native naturalists with whom I was on friendly terms, lastly, to the Government, but all in vain. The reply was 'The penalty of death is inflicted on anyone who may export these eggs.' Another idea then possessed me; to apply to one of my pupils. As the Principal of the Imperial School of Medicine at Nagasaki, I was surrounded with students from the different provinces of Japan, and amongst others from the provinces of Echizen and Vigo, or Hiogo, where alone the *Yama-mai* silkworms are reared. One of these youths, who had on several occasions given me proofs of his extraordinary devotion, was selected by me for the purpose; to him I explained the whole affair, and proposed that he should go to Vigo at my expense, in order to collect and send me as many eggs as possible. This brave young man, whose name I have promised never to divulge, started on the morrow, and after an absence of 15 days secretly sent me the eggs, which he had collected with much difficulty and danger to himself. He told me that no one suspected the object of his journey; that was in October 1862. My mission to Japan was finished November 1st, 1862. I started for Europe by the English mail packet, and undertook the charge of carrying these eggs to Europe. This was by no means an easy matter on board a steam ship in the Tropics. If the eggs were kept in the cabin, a great risk of their premature hatching was incurred, for the temperature there in the month of November is above 95° F., and in the Red Sea 105° and more. I followed the advice of M. Simon, and placed the eggs in an ice box on board ship, though often but little ice was therein. To this precaution is due, in a great measure, their safe arrival in Europe in good condition. I arrived at the Hague early in January 1863, and at once sent out the eggs. The greater part were sent to the French Government and to the Imperial Society of Acclimatisation, according to promise I had made to my friend M. Simon."

ACTIAS SELENE, OR PHALAENA ATTACUS.

This species feeds on the *Munsooree* (*Coriaria nipalensis*), The cocoon is enclosed between two leaves. The silk does not appear to be windable, but it is of a coarseish kind and might be spun if it could be obtained in sufficient quantity. It is very desirable that the applicability of this silk be investigated.

In addition to the *Munsooree* this worm feeds on the wild cherry and walnut. The diameter of the cocoon fibre is, as will be seen in the table, page 68, $\frac{1}{1000}$ of an inch, and it has about an average strength and tension, and thus presents no obstacle to its use. The cocoon is rather large, being 3 inches long and 1¼ inches in diameter. The entomology is illustrated in Plates XIII. and XIV.

ATTACUS EDWARDSIA.

In the Indian Museum there are two specimens of an *Atlas* moth, from Darjeeling, of an intensely dark colour, and possessing sufficient structural divergence from *Attacus Atlas* to warrant Mr. Moore's affirming it to be a distinct species. It has been named *Attacus Edwardsia.* Mr. Gosse has the following interesting note respecting it :—

As Darjeeling is 7,000 feet above the level of the sea, and has a climate in which rain and snow are abundant in winter and humidity is constant, it surely would be not difficult to acclimatise this noble form (be it variety or species) in the British Isles.*

ANTHERÆA PEROTTETI.

This is described by Mr. Geoghegan as producing a strong, wiry, and brilliant silk, but requires carding. The larvæ feed, in captivity, on the *Odina wodier* (Roxb.). "Undergoes four moults and yields four crops a year." Fishing lines of this silk are said to be made in Dinapoor.

ANTHERÆA ROYLEI.

Is described by the same author as being found in Darjeeling, and in the Himalayas from Kumaon to the Punjaub, and feeds on *Quercus incana*. The silk is good, but not abundant, and the insect can be domesticated. Yields two or three crops a year.

Plate VII. Fig. 1, illustrates the entomology of this species.

BOMBYX TEXTOR.

This species, known as the "*Pat*" silkworm, is found in Assam. It feeds on the mulberry tree, and is probably a variety of *Bombyx mori*, the cocoons being of the same yellow colour, although somewhat different in shape.

The diameter of the fibre of the silk produced from this worm is $\frac{1}{2500}$ in., as fine as the silk of *B. mori*.

A Government Report gives the following particulars concerning it:—

"The '*Pat*' gives only one crop of cocoons in the year. In Upper Assam the eggs are hatched about the end of December, and in Lower Assam about the end of January. The worm is more delicate and has to be treated with more care than the *Eria*. The silk is, however, more valuable. Great care has to be taken to keep everything about the '*Pat*' scrupulously clean."

CRICULA TRIFENESTRATA.

Very abundant in British Burmah, where the cocoons rot in the jungles for want of gathering. The silk of this species promises to be most useful, and only waits importation to Europe and utilization. It is a strong, rich, and glossy silk. See also pp. 7, 68, 85, and 126.

---

* Gosse's "Life-history of Attacus Atlas," p. 6.

CHAPTER XIV.

LIFE-HISTORY OF SEVERAL SILK-PRODUCING WORMS, and TABLE of the diameter, strength, and tension of a single fibre, and dimensions of cocoon, of the chief Mulberry and Indian Wild Silks.

The following table of the life-history of several of the chief silk-producing worms is given in a Government report:—

Name of Silkworm.	Period of Life of Moth.	Period from their laying of Eggs to their being hatched.	Period of Life of Moth.	Period from Beginning of Worm to spin to Completion of Chrysalis.	From Completion of Chrysalis to Emergence of Moth from Cocoon.
Tussar or Kulkuri	3 or 4 days.	9 days	36 days	15 days	—
Moonga	6 days	10 days	30 days	5 or 6 days	16 to 20 days
Eria	Not known exactly. A complete cycle is made in from 43 days to 2 months.				
Pat major, or Bombyx textor; Pat minor, or Bombyx eræsi	3 or 4 days.	10 months	30 to 40 days	5 or 6 days	20 to 25 days

TABLE of the Diameter, Strength, and Tension of a single Fibre and Dimensions of Cocoon of the chief Mulberry and Indian Wild Silks.

Name of Worm or Silk.	Country.	Diameter in fractions of an inch.		Tension or limit of stretch before breaking in inches of single Fibre one Foot long.		Strength of single Fibre in drams avoirdupois.		Dimensions of Cocoons in inches.
		Outside of Cocoon.	Inner part of Cocoon.	Outside of Cocoon.	Inner part of Cocoon.	Outside of Cocoon.	Inner part of Cocoon.	
Bombyx mori, or mulberry silk	China	$\frac{1}{2150}$	$\frac{1}{2150}$	1¼	1¾	2⅜	2⅞	1½ × ½
	Italy	$\frac{1}{2150}$	$\frac{1}{2100}$	1	1¾	2⅝	2⅞	1¼ × ⅝
	Japan	$\frac{1}{1800}$	$\frac{1}{1650}$	1	1¾	2¾	2⅞	1¼ × ⅝
	Bengal	$\frac{1}{2000}$	$\frac{1}{2200}$	1¼	1⅓	2⅛	2⅜	1⅛ × ⅝
Bombyx textor	India	$\frac{1}{2800}$	$\frac{1}{2500}$	1¼	1⅓	2¼	2⅓	1¼ × 1⅛
Antheræa mylitta, or Tusser silk.	„	$\frac{1}{770}$	$\frac{1}{710}$	1	1	7	8	1½ × ⅞
Attacus ricini, or Eria silk.	„	$\frac{1}{1500}$	$\frac{1}{1430}$	1	1⅓	1⅞	2⅓	1½ × ¾
Attacus Cynthia, or Ailanthus silk.	„	$\frac{1}{1250}$	$\frac{1}{1230}$	1	1½	2¼	2½	1¼ × ¾
Anstheræa Assama, or Muga silk.	„	$\frac{1}{1430}$	$\frac{1}{1080}$	1	¾	2⅛	3	1¾ × 1
Actias selene	„	$\frac{1}{1000}$	$\frac{1}{1100}$	1	1¼	2	2¼	3 × 1¼
Attacus atlas	„	$\frac{1}{1320}$	$\frac{1}{1000}$	1	1¼	2⅛	2½	3½ × ⅞
Antheræa yama-mai	Japan	$\frac{1}{1000}$	$\frac{1}{1000}$	¾	1	2⅛	3	1½ × ⅞
Cricula trifenestrata	India	—	$\frac{1}{850}$	—	—	—	—	2 × ¾

CHAPTER XV.

MOTHS' SCALES.

Under the microscope, the dust-like particles which are removed by the finger when the moth's wing is touched are more or less triangular-shaped plates pointed at the end of their attachment to the membrane of the wing, and widening out at the extremity of their lengths into either serrated edges, as in the case of *Antheræa yama-mai*, Plate L., Figs. 5 and 6, or long digitate processes or spikes, as in *Actias Selene*, Plate L., Fig. 4, giving in the various species a most interesting variety of shapes, from the narrow fusiform appearance in *Attacus Cynthia*, Plate XLIX., Fig. 5, to the broad scales of the Tusser moth, Plate XLIX., Figs. 2 and 3, which are not unlike the shape of a bat-wing burner. The scales, as they rest in situ on the moth's wing, overlap each other with great regularity, like the tiles of a roof, and somewhat analogous to the imbrications observable under the microscope in the fur and wool of many animals. I have had drawings made of the scales of some of the species the silk of which is likely to come into more or less extended use.

The first 24 diagrams have been drawn from the microscopic appearance of the scales when magnified 140 diameters, all being taken from that part of the moth's wing indicated in Plate XXIII., Fig. 2, except the following:—

Bombyx mori (Plate LII. Fig. 3).
Actias Selene „ „ 6).
Antheræa mylitta „ „ 4).
Antheræa yama-mai (Plate LII. Fig. 5).

The scales represented in these four diagrams are taken indiscriminately from all parts of the wing.

The object of this inquiry is to show the structual differences of the scales of the various species of the Indian silk-producing *Lepidoptera*. I cannot say that I have discovered sufficient divergence in form corresponding with specific differences in the moths, but there is no doubt such divergence is very wide, and sufficient to distinguish the genus *Attacus* from that of *Antheræa*.

The size of the scales is not in proportion to the size of the moths, as may be seen from the scales of *Antheræa mylitta* being broader than those of *Attacus Atlas*, although the expanse of wing in the Atlas moth is 4 to 5 inches more than in *Antheræa mylitta.* There is, however, a curious correspondence between the scales of the moth *Antheræa mylitta*, which are the largest, and the fibre spun by its larva, which is the coarsest, and between the scales of the moth *Bombyx mori*, which are the smallest, and the fibre spun by its lava, which is the finest.

In some of the species the difference between the scale of the male and those of the female is considerable. In *Antheræa mylitta* the extremities of the scales of the male are much more digitate, whilst in the female they are simply serrated. In *Antheræa yama-mai* the scales of the male appear to be broader and shorter than of the female. The greatest divergence, however, is in the case of our English moorland species, *Saturnia carpini*, or the Emperor moth (Plate LI., Fig. 2). The scales of the male bear some resemblance in shape to those of *Bombyx mori*, whilst those of the female have extremely long spikes at the two outside edges, forming horn-like processes.

The bodies of the moths are generally covered with downy hairs, becoming in some species very long at the inner extremities of the wings.

I have had drawings made of the scales of twelve species much more highly magnified, to ascertain their structural differences. I have taken a single scale of each of the twelve species from the part of the wing indicated in Plate XXIII., Fig. 2, and magnified it 500 diameters (*see* Plates LIII. and LIV.)

APPENDIX I.

The Indian Silkworm, from the Annual Report of the Government Central Museum, Bombay, for the year 1859–60.—By Dr. Birdwood, C.S.I.

In paragraph 18 of last year's report I mentioned the steps taken up to that date for the cultivation of the indigenous silkworm of the Deccan. As therein stated, my attention was first drawn to this subject by Mr. Heycock, at the meeting held in the Town Hall on the 15th December 1858, for the purpose of founding the Victoria Museum and gardens. Mr. Heycock said that, during an excursion to Bassein made by him in the preceding month, he entered the house of a friend who until lately had resided in Bengal, and who had collected a number of silkworms in his garden gathered off the "Wild Plum" of the surrounding jungle. His friend told Mr. Heycock that the Tusseh silk of Bengal was produced by these worms, but that in this Presidency no one knew what they were, and they were left to be devoured, and their cocoons were wasted. From a cocoon obligingly given to me by Mr. Heycock I found that I was very familiar with it in the parts of the Deccan in which I had been stationed, although ignorant of its value. I had often seen the worm feeding on the leaves of the *Blair* tree (*Zizyphus Jujuba*) during the cold season about Sholapoor, and had noticed that its cocoons appeared about October and November, and that the moth burst from them about July, when it immediately laid its eggs, which were hatched in one or two weeks. In bringing these facts to the notice of Government, in a letter, No. 193, of December 31st, 1858, I suggested that should it be deemed desirable to introduce the rearing of silkworms into this Presidency, one or two hundred Tusseh cocoons should be procured from Bengal, and distributed throughout this Presidency, with the view of determining whether identical species of cocoons were to be found in the Presidency, and in what collectorate; and that should it appear from this investigation that the production of silk can be undertaken in any of the collectorates of this Presidency, a few ryots from Bengal, acquainted with the mode of rearing the worms and off-reeling their cocoons, with perhaps one or two silk weavers, should be brought round to Bombay to introduce this new industry to our ryots, and at first through the instrumentality of the jails. Government, having approved of the proposed measures, sent to Bengal for the Tusseh cocoons; and these, having arrived in this port in October 1859, were distributed in the following November to all the collectors under the Presidency, excepting those of Rutnagherry and Belgaum, with the circular No. 2791 of 1859, General Department. The Bengal cocoons are those of the *Saturnia Mylitta,* and indentical with those shown to me by Mr. Heycock and found by me at Sholapoor, the Bombay *Paphia* to which I had attributed the Deccan cocoons being the same moth as the *Saturnia Mylitta,* under another name. *Saturnia Mylitta* of Bengal is found there, on the Blair tree.

But Bengalees, it seems, distinguish between the cocoons found on the Blair and those cocoons found on the Asseen tree. The former they call *Bughy,* the latter *Jarro,* and the latter they deem the better sort. The Asseen of Bengal is the *ain, aeen, ayen* of this Presidency, the *Terminalia glabra* vel *alata* vel *Pentaptera tomentosa* of botanists, found throughout Goozerat and the Coucans, on which the worm has been noticed to feed in these countries by Dr. Gibson, and by Mr. Bellasis, the collector of Surat.

During the last three weeks I have found the cocoons of the *Saturnia Mylitta* on the Komba or Kumber of this island, the *Careya arborea* of botanists, a handsome tree of the myrtle kind, a native of the Coucans, Goozerat, and Khandeish. The only collectorate from which I have yet had reply to last year's circular is that of Surat, where Mr. Bellasis wishes to have a Bengal ryot sent at once.

The Agri-Horticultural Society of Western India, and a private merchant of Bombay, are also anxious to have the services of expert Bengalees placed at their disposal.

The cultivation of the worm is an easy matter. When they abound and are accessible, it is sufficient merely to protect them and their eggs from the depredation of birds. If not abundant, or not accessible, nurseries of Blair or Ayen trees should be raised for them, and, if by Government, in connection with the jails. A few trees only are necessary, as the worms can spin just as well in frames as on the branches of trees. If a supply of leaves can be kept up by irrigation, the worms will probably spin all the year round, as in Bengal, instead of only after the rains.

Reeling off the cocoons is a delicate task, but when once

learnt it can be done with the coarsest machinery, as will appear from the account given of silk reeling in a work recently received from Europe, entitled—"Twelve Years in China: the People, the Rebels, and the Mandarins." It has been objected that any attempt to introduce the cultivation of silk here will be very expensive, that there is little chance of its succeeding, and that it should be left to private enterprise and not be undertaken by Government. It is forgotten, however, in urging the first objection, that the experiments now recommended are not for the naturalisation of a foreign worm, but simply for the utilisation of an indigenous species. Signor Mutti's experiments near Poona, in 1838, were for the purpose of introducing the China mulberry and the China worm into this country, and they cost Rs. 2,00,000 and failed utterly. The worm now proposed to be utilised is already naturalised, with its food, and it only has to be protected against the enemies which at present naturally check its increase. Shield it from these, and in all likelihood it will multiply here in unlimitable quantity. But notwithstanding the *Saturnia Mylitta* is indigenous to Western India, and that silk rearing and reeling would in all likelihood become a very popular industry with the natives of this Presidency under ordinary circumstances, it would still be unsafe to predict positively of the results of the experiment I recommended last year. Bengal is too far away to afford any argument for anticipating the success of cocoon-rearing here. Fortunately, however, the experiment has been tried at our own doors with every good fortune. From a letter No. 401 of January 1860, received by me, as Secretary of the Agri-Horticultural Society of Western India, from Captain C. P. Maloney, Secretary to the General Committee of the Madras Exhibition of 1859, it appears that the rearing of silkworms, the preparation of raw silk, dyed and undyed, and the manufacture of silk stuffs from the *Saturnia Mylitta*, is carried on to a very great extent in the territories of his Highness the Nizam.

The report on the industry received by the Madras Committee is from Syed Mohdeen Padshah, talookdar of Wurrangal. In the hot season, in the months of Chittur (April) and Visak (May), the *Tussah* chrysalis is little larger than a pigeon's egg.

In the season when they gather the flowers of the Mowah (*Bassia latifolia*) the people search for the Tusseh cocoons in the jungles, and find them on the Blair and Muddi or Arichunmugay (*Ayeen*) trees. Tying them in bundles they hang them up in their houses with great care. When the thunder comes the moths burst from the cocoous, the male moth being red and the female yellow. The female moths, in numbers from two to 20, are placed in baskets lined with tar (*Borassus flabelliformis*) and teak (*Tectona grandis*) leaves, and plastered on the outside with cow-dung.

After nine or 10 days each moth deposits from 50 to 200 eggs, resembling grains of *Jowaree* slightly flattened, and then dies. During the breeding season the experts (*Nykavarram* and *Rosawaram*) in charge of the worms fast! The eggs are kept in the baskets from eight to 10 days, when the young caterpillars appear.

These are carried into the jungle and placed on Muddi (*Ayeen*) and (*Chungay*) (?) trees, the trunks of which are surrounded with ashes to keep off ants. People are also kept in the neighbourhood to frighten away kites, crows, and other animals of prey.

When the caterpillars have devoured all the leaves, baskets are made of rousa grass (*Andropogon calamus aromaticus*) lined with Muddi (*Ayeen*) and (*Chungay*) (?) leaves, and the caterpillars are placed in them and hung up among the branches of the trees. There they are left for two months, after which the worms begin to weave their cocoons. In preparing the Tusseh silk the cocoons are first steamed with water, to which various ingredients have been added to promote the solution of the substance which holds together the fibres of the cocoons.

The cocoons are then dried and then again placed in pure water, when, one of their fibres being drawn out, they are reeled off on an instrument made for the purpose similar to an ordinary spinning wheel.

Seyd Mohdeen states that from 300 to 800 cocoons are sold for a rupee, while Tusseh silk fetches from 10 to 12 rupees a seer and a half undyed.

If dyed it costs a rupee per every 5 to 8 tolas. He gives receipts for all the dyes, and adds that three crops of cocoon can be obtained in a year, although he has only followed out the history of the hot-season crop.

There can be no doubt now that this industry would prove very remunerative throughout the Deccan, especially as we should here dispense with the costly experts employed during the breeding of the moths by the Nizam's people, probably for purely superstitious reasons. Their fasting looks, however, as if the industry were attended with some risks, something to be prayed against.

The employment of Roossa grass baskets at a later stage has also probably a superstitious significance.

The interest of Government in the matter extends only to introducing the industry to the notice of the Deccan ryots; when they have once been made acquainted with its value, Government will leave it to be carried on as a commercial speculation. Every Government must necessarily have a direct concern in adding to the exchangeable products of its subjects. When the latter are on an equality as regards intelligence and civilisation with their rulers, the national prosperity is in sufficiently safe-keeping and may wisely be left entirely in their hands. But when it unfortunately happens that a Government is far ahead of its people in intelligence and civilisation, as in this country, it is bound to directly interest itself, to a certain extent, in any practicable and moderate scheme which may be proposed for their material benefit. In concluding this subject, I would beg to add that it would be probably unadvisable to carry the preparation of the cocoons in this Presidency beyond the stage of undyed raw silk.

The best books on the Tusseh moth are Jardine's Naturalist's Library Volume, "Sastic Moths." "Remarks on the Silk Worms of Assam," by Thomas Hugon, in the 6th vol. of the Journal of the Asiatic Society of Bengal. "On the Indigenous Moths of India," by Dr. Helfer, in the same volume. "Account of the Tusseh and Arindy Silk Worms of Bengal," by Dr. W. Roxburgh, in vol. 7 of the Transactions of the Linnæan Society. "Silk Culture in India," at page 115 of Royle's "Reproductive Resources of India." "Account of the Silk Trade and Silk Manufactures of the Punjab," in part 2, vol. 10, of the Journal of the Agricultural and Horticultural Society of India. There is also a report of the proceedings of the East India Company in regard to the trade, culture, and manufacture of raw silk, published in 1836, which I have not yet seen, and on the experiments formerly instituted for the introduction of silk culture into this Presidency there is Signor Mulli's "Guide to the Silk Culture in the Deccan," printed in 1838, in English, Goozerattee, and Mahrattee, and a pamphlet "On the introduction of Silk, and the Cultivation of the "Mulberry under the Bombay Presidency for the Agri-"Horticultural Society of Western India," by Dr. Charles Lush, formerly superintendent of the Government Gardens at Dapooree. Reference to the subject is also made in the following reports of the Chamber of Commerce of Bombay:—

			Page
Report for 1838		- - - -	8
„	1839–40, first quarter	-	15
„	„ „ second „	- -	12–15
„	„ „ third „	- - -	10
„	„ „ fourth „	- -	111
„	1840–41, „ „	- - -	10
„	1841–42, „ „	- -	18
„	1842–43, third „	- -	11
„	„ „ first „	- -	7
„	1843–44, second „	- -	12
„	„ „ third „	- - -	7
„	„ „ fourth „	- -	11
„	1844–45, first „	- -	7
„	„ „ fourth „	- - -	13
„	1845–46, second and third quarters		12
„	1846–47, „		10

APPENDIX II.

TABLE of Indian Coins, Weights, and Measures.*

Money.

Silver is the legally constituted medium of exchange in all money transactions throughout all the British Indian Possessions. Gold coin was intended to be a legal tender, at a fixed value of 16 rupees for the gold mohur of Calcutta, and 15 rupees for the gold rupee of Madras and Bombay; but it is not demandable in payment, and is left to find its current value in the market.

			Value sterling.		
			£	s.	d.
		1 Pie	0	0	$0\frac{1}{8}$
3 Pie	=	1 Piasa or $\frac{1}{4}$ Anna	0	0	$0\frac{3}{8}$
12 Pie	=	1 Anna	0	0	$1\frac{1}{2}$
16 Annas	=	1 Rupee	0	2	0
15 Rupees	=	1 Gold Rupee	1	10	0
16 Rupees	=	1 Gold Mohar	1	12	0
100,000 Rupees	=	1 Lakh	10,000	0	0
100 Lakhs	=	1 Karor	1,000,000	0	0

---

* From "Times of India Calendar and Directory," 1870.

The value of a rupee is generally assumed as equal to 2*s.* sterling. At the Calcutta mint price of silver it is worth 2*s.* 0·035*d.*; at the commercial par of exchange, 1*s.* 11·51*d.*; and at the London mint price of silver it is worth 1*s.* 11·04*d.*

The rupee weighs 180 grains troy, or one tola, and consists of 11 parts of silver and one of alloy. The gold rupee is of the same weight and standard. The copper coins are the half anna, weighing 200 grains; the quarter anna or paisa, 100 grains; the half paisa, 50 grains; and the pie, 33⅓ grains.

In Bombay, accounts are still often kept in rupees, quarters, and raes, 25 raes making one anna.

In Madras, accounts were formerly kept in Star Pagodas, fanams, and cash.

80 Cash = 1 Fanam or panam.
42 Fanams = 1 Star Pagoda, Hum or Varaha.

The Pagoda was of gold 19½ carats fine, and intrinsically worth 7*s.* 5¼*d.*

1.—*Bombay Local Weights.*

4 Dhan or yav	= 1 Raktica or Gunj	2·1267 gr. tr.	·01182 tola
8 Raktica	= 1 Masha	8·5069 ,,	·09452 ,,
4 Masha	= 1 Tank	2·4889 dr. av.	·37809 ,,
72 Tank, or 30 pa'is	= 1 Ser	11⅕ oz. av.	27⅑ ,,
40 Sers	= 1 Man	28 lb. av.	1088⅑ ,,
20 Mans	= 1 Khandi	560 lb. av.	6·8056 Imp. man.

The Khandi for Cotton is 28 mans or 784 lbs. avoir. or 7 cwt.

The "pakka ser" is $1\frac{13}{15}$ lbs. avoir., or 72·59 tolas. At Panwel the ser weighs 72·83 tolas.

The British Indian or Imperial ser and man are 2·9387755 Bombay sers and mans respectively; and the Bombay man is 0·3402778 Imperial mans.

The Bombay ser weighs 317·51485 grammes, and the man 12·700594 kilogrammes.

Poona.

The ser is 80 Ankushi rupees or 76·66 standard tolas, or 1·9714 lbs avoir., or 2·33604 lbs. troy = ·9583 B. I. seers.

The weights are the same as the British Indian, only one 24th part lighter.

4½ Tanks	= 1 Chhatank	1·9714 oz. av.	0·958 Imp. chhat.
4 Chhatanks	= 1 Pau-ser	7·8856 ,,	3·833 ,,
4 Paua	= 1 Ser	1·9714 lb. av.	0·958 Imp. Ser.
5 Sers	= 1 Passeri	9·857 ,,	4·791 ,,
8 Paserri	= 1 Man	78·856 ,,	38·329 ,,
3 Mans or 120 Ser	= 1 Palla	23·657 ,,	2·875 Imp. Man.
6⅔ Pallas (20 Mans)	= 1 Khandi	1577·12 ,,	19·165 ,,

Kachcha mans of 12½ and 14 sers are also used in the district.

In the Khed, Purandhar, and Bhimathadi talukas the ser weighs 76 tolas; in Shiwner and Indapur, 76½; in Pabal, 77; and in Mawal, 75 tolas.

Ahmadnagar and Sholapur.

The British Indian or Imperial weights are in use.

At Ahmadnagar the Palla is 2½ mans.

At Sholapur: 1 Manki = 4 dharas = 12 sers.

Satara.

The ser varies in different localities from 92·75 tolas at Koley to 115 tolas at Mamdapur. In Satara city it is 93·25 tolas.

Sindh.

The British Indian weights were declared by proclamation 1st August 1853 to be the only legal standard.

8 mans = 1 khandi = 658$\frac{2}{7}$ lbs. av. = 23·510204 Bombay mans.

Surat.

The Surat ser of 35 Surat tolas is variously stated from 36·4583 to 37 tolas, and the man from 37½ to 38 lbs. avoirdupois, the former being probably the more accurate determination, from which—

1 Surat ser	=	·455729	British Indian sers.
1 „	=	1·339286	Bombay „
1 British Indian ser	=	2·1942857	Surat „
1 Bombay „	=	·746667	Surat „

The Khandi for Cotton is 21 mans, or 7 cwt. 3½ lbs.

Khandesh, &c.

The British Indian system is authorised in these districts.

Broach, &c.

At Broach the ser is	40	tolas.
„ Ahmod „ „	38·5	„
„ Jambusar and Anklesar	38	„
„ Wagra	37·5	„
„ Hansot	38·8125	

Madras.

10 Pagodas	= 1 Palam	$1\frac{1}{4}$ oz. avoir.	3·038 tolas
8 Pollums	= 1 Ser	$\frac{5}{8}$ lb. „	24·304 „
5 Sers	= 1 Vis	$3\frac{1}{8}$ lb. „	121·528 „
8 Vis or 40 Sers	= 1 Man	25 lb. „	972·222 „
20 Mans	= 1 Khandi	500 lb. „	6·0764 Imp. mans.

The Madras man is 0·303819 British Indian mans, and the British Indian or Imperial man is 3·2914286 Madras mans; 1 Bombay man = 1·12 Madras mans, and 1 Madras man = 0·892857 Bombay man. The Madras man is sometimes stated at 30 lbs. troy or 0·3 British Indian man, equal to 24·6857143 lbs. avoir., which makes the Palam exactly 3 tolas and the khandi 6 British Indian mans.

The Mangelin for pearls is 6 grains. 18 Madras Chows= 55 Bombay Chows.

The Pagoda Weight = 52·56 grains.

6.—*Measures of Time.*

		1 Pal	24 seconds.
60	Pal	= 1 Ghari	24 minutes.
$7\frac{1}{2}$	Ghari	= 1 Pahar, or prahar	3 hours.
8	Pahar or 60 ghari	= 1 Din	1 day.
7	Din	= 1 Hafta	1 week.
30	Din	= 1 Mahina	1 month.
12	Mahina	= 1 Baras	1 year.

The Hindus reckon by a lunar year for religious, and by a sidereal year for civil purposes.

	days	hrs.	min.	seconds.
The exact length of the sidereal year	365	6	9	19·6
By the Surya Siddhanta it is	365	6	12	36·56
By the Arya Siddhanta „	365	6	12	30
By the Brahma Siddhanta „	365	6	12	9
By the Parasara Siddhanta „	365	6	12	31·4

And since the Gregorian year has an average length of 365d. 5h. 49m. 12s. the Hindu year = 1·000042 Gregorian years.

The Gregorian year = 0·999958 Hindu years. The year of the Surya Siddhanta = 1·000045286 mean solar years, or one day in excess in 60·46 years.

1.—The following are some of the principal Foreign Gold Coins, with their approximate values in Rupees, reckoning gold at 15 times the value of silver of the same degree of purity.

Gold Coins.	Weight in Grains.	Standard.	Value. Rs. a. p.
British Sovereign	123·274	916⅔	10 4 4
German Ducat	53·89	986	4 13 3
French Napoleon of 20 francs	99·545	900	8 2 4
Russian ½ Imperial of 5 roubles	101·005	916	8 6 8
Persian Gold Rupee	—	—	14 15 6
Italian Pistole of Pius VI.	84·43	917	7 0 7
Persian Toman	73·0	971	6 6 0
Double Eagle of the United States 20 dollars	515·98	900	42 3 4
Madras Star Pagoda	52·40	812	3 14 2

2.—Intrinsic Value of the principal Foreign Silver Coins.

Silver Coins.	Weight in Grains.	Standard.	Value. Rs. a. p.
Great Britain.			
Crown	436·36	925	2 7 1½
Florin	174·55	—	0 15 8
Shilling	87·27	—	0 7 10
Persia.			
Rupee of Shiraz, A.H. 1245–1248	105·12	916⅔	0 9 4
Larin of Persia and Arabia	74·5	965	0 6 11½
India.			
Timasha of Nipal	34·3	929	3 0 1
Rupee of Nipal 1808–1824, average	84·7	768	0 6 4
Madras half pagoda	326·73	894	12 1 3
„ 5 Fanam	71·51	900	6 0 3
Goa rupee	168·5	864	0 14 1½

APPENDIX III.

CATALOGUE of the Collection of WILD SILKS in the Indian Section, South Kensington Museum.

1. Eggs of *Antheræa mylitta*, or Tusser moth.
2. Drawing of Tusser silkworm, *Antheræa mylitta* (Linnæus), natural size, full-grown.

Synonyms :—

Bombyx mylitta (Fabricius).
Attacus mylitta (Blanchard).
Saturnia paphia (Helfer).

3. Moths and cocoons of the Tusser silkworm, *Antheræa mylitta* (Linnæus).
4. Tusser silk moths hatched at Leek from cocoons sent to Mr. T. Wardle, by Major Coussmaker, from Poonah. The cocoons are shown below the moths.
5. Tusser moth and its pierced cocoon, showing filaments of silk.
6. Cocoons of the Tusser silkworm with pedicles, some of which show portions of the branches to which they were attached.
7. Tusser cocoons cut open to show the chrysalis or pupa inside each.
8. Tusser cocoons from which the moths have emerged at the pierced ends, with pedicles showing mode of attachment to branches from which the worm forms its cocoon.
9. Tusser cocoon cut open to show the compact interior, and also a portion of it pulled out to show the silky filaments of which it is composed.
10. Tusser cocoon showing the filaments of silk drawn out from the pierced end, and the mode in which the silk is deposited.
11. Native-reeled Tusser silk and reeling implements.
12. Tusser raw silk, native reeled with native reeling implements from Bhagulpore, Hazareebagh.
13. Waste Tusser silk from Tamba, Bombay.
14. Tusser Tram unbleached. Tusser Tram bleached, showing result of the new mode of removing the brown colouring matter from the silk.
15. Improved reeled Tusser raw silk, also Organzine and Tram, with one specimen bleached, in the following order :—

16 hanks of Tusser raw silk, reeled in Italy, showing the improvements in reeling of which Tusser is susceptible. Size, 23 to 27 deniers, or 1½ drams per 1,000 yards.

9 hanks of Tusser Organzine (warp), made of the above improved Tusser raw. Size, 52 deniers, or 1,000 yards, weighing 3 drams.

1 hank of the above Tusser Organzine, bleached by the improved process, and ready for dyeing.

12 hanks of Tusser Tram (weft), made of the above improved Tusser raw. Size, 52 deniers, or 1,000 yards weighing 3 drams.

16. Native rudely dyed Tusser silk from Azimgurh.

17. Series of Tusser Organzine and Tram in skeins, for weaving, dyed with European dyes, chiefly aniline, to show the capability of this silk for modern commercial dyes (*petits teints*), illustrative of the improved application of commercial dyes by Mr. T. Wardle.

18. Second series of Tusser Organzine, European dyes, as above.

19. Tusser silk for weaving (Organzine and Tram, 52 deniers) of the improved reeling, and dyed.

The dyes are modern, chiefly aniline, to show the capability of this silk to receive the modern commercial dyes (not permanent, "*petits teints*"), as improved by Mr. T. Wardle.

20. Skeins of German dyed Tusser silk for weaving.

21. Frame of Tusser net silk fabrics, cocoon reeled English manufacture, natural colour, undyed, plain.

22. Frame of Tusser net silk fabrics, cocoon reeled English manufacture, natural colour, undyed, figured.

23. Frame of Tusser net silk fabrics, cocoon reeled, English manufacture, natural colour, undyed, figured.

24. Frame of Tusser Schappe or spun silk fabric, woven in figured designs, undyed.

25. Frame of Tusser Schappe or spun silk fabrics, woven in figured designs, undyed.

26. Frame of Tusser Schappe or spun silk fabrics, woven in figured designs, undyed.

27. Furniture cloth, undyed Tusser silk, figured weaving.

28. Piece of Tusser silk, ornamental weaving, French.

29. Frame of Tusser printed silk cloth, native woven, designed by W. Morris, Esq., M.A., printed by Mr. T. Wardle.

30. Frame of Tusser printed silk cloth, native woven, designed by W. Morris, Esq., M.A., printed by Mr. T. Wardle.

31. Frame of Tusser printed silk cloth, native woven, designed by W. Morris, Esq., M.A., printed by Mr. T. Wardle.

32. Frame of Tusser printed silk cloth, native woven, designed by W. Morris, Esq., M.A., printed by Mr. T. Wardle.

33. Printed Tusser silk cloth.

34. Printed Tusser silk cloth.

35. Six prints on Tusser cloth, printed with Indian colours and designs.

36. Two pieces French woven Tusser silk with dyed stripes of Italian silk.

37. Piece of Tusser silk dyed black and printed in gold.

38. Piece of Tusser silk dyed red and printed in gold.

39. Large Tusser silk cloth palampore, printed with Indian colour and design.

40. Large Tusser silk cloth palampore, native woven, printed in Indian designs in centre, with lotus border.

41. Shawl of Tusser silk and wool.

42. Union Tusser silk scarfs, made of dyed and undyed Tusser silk with a little admixture of mulberry silk.

43. Black Tusser silk plush. The first utilisation of this silk to a pile surface, made as an experiment in Germany in 1879.

44. Tusser silk plush, called "Seal Cloth," made of Tusser spun silk. The new and important English manufacture of 1880.

45. Fichu or shawl, made with Tusser spun yarn.

46. Specimen of furniture silk, woven in design, undyed. English.

47. The new Tusser embroidery, "Tusser on Tusser," worked with Tusser silk floss on ground of Tusser silk cloth; Indian designs; floss dyed with Indian dyestuffs; 11 borders. Executed by the Leek Embroidery School. Lent by Mrs. Wardle, Honorary Superintendent.

48. Tusser cocoons, called also Tasar, Tusseh, Tussah, and Tussore.

49. Tusser floss silk for embroidery; series of colours dyed with Indian dyestuffs.

50. Chair cover, No. 1, "Tusser on Tusser." Embroidered from Indian designs with Tusser floss on native woven Tusser silk cloth. Floss dyed with Indian dyestuffs by T. Wardle. Executed by the Leek School of Embroidery; the colouring by Mrs. Wardle, Honorary Superintendent.

51. Pulpit cloth, Tusser embroidery on silk velvet. Executed by the Leek School of Embroidery; the colouring by Mrs. Wardle, Honorary Superintendent.

52. Chair cover, No. 2, "Tusser on Tusser." Embroidered from Indian designs with Tusser floss on native woven Tusser silk cloth. Floss dyed with Indian dyestuffs by T. Wardle. Executed by the Leek School of Embroidery; the colouring by Mrs. Wardle, Honorary Superintendent.

53. Moths and cocoons of the Eria or Arindy silkworm, *Attacus ricini.*

54. Frame of dried leaves of some of the plants on which the Tusser and Eria silkworms feed, viz.:—

Tusser, *Terminalia catappa.*
„ *Pentaptera tomentosa* (deciduous).
„ *Tectona grandis.*
„ *Elccæcaria insignis, L.* (*Falconeria,* Royle).
„ *Shorea robusta.*
Eria, *Ricinus communis.*

55. Eria cocoons.

56. Eria silk, Assam, as rudely spun ready for weaving by the natives.

57. Twenty-eight skeins of Eria silk, native dyed.

58. English carded Eria silk of *Attacus ricini,* 1st draft, showing its beautiful fibre.

59. Four hanks of Eria spun yarn (not reeled), 30/2 (*i.e.,* 30 skeins of 800 yards each per lb.), showing the highly improved state of yarn by English spinning machinery.

60. Fourteen colours of dyed Eria schappe or spun silk, aniline dyes, for commerce.

61. Eria Schappe or spun silk (not reeled), 16/2 fold, dyed with Indian dyestuffs, five colours.

62. Brown Eria Schappe or spun silk (not reeled), 16/2 fold for "seal cloth" plush.

63. Eria silk cloth, native home spun and woven (to show the roughness of the cloth).

64. Eria silk cloth, from improved English spinning, undyed, quite new, woven in figured designs.

65. Eria silk cloth, from improved English spinning. undyed, quite new, woven in various designs.

66. Five pieces of Eria cloth, printed by Mr. T. Wardle from designs of W. Morris, Esq., M.A.

67. Muga or Moonga silk cocoons, *Antheræa Assama,* Durang, Assam.

68. Moths of the Muga silkworm, *Antheræa Assama.*

69. Three skeins of Muga reeled raw silk.

70. One skein of Muga silk in the "boiled off" or discharged state, and ready to be dyed.

71. Six skeins of Muga silk, native dyed, Assam.

72. Carded Muga silk, showing its beautiful fibre.

73. Cloth of Muga spun silk, undyed.

74. One piece of Muga spun silk or Schappe woven in figured design, undyed.

75. Cloth of Muga spun silk, printed by Mr. T. Wardle, design by W. Morris, Esq., M.A.

76. Five pieces of Muga spun cloth, printed by Mr. T. Wardle, designs by W. Morris, Esq., M.A.

77. Silk from the cocoon of *Cricula trifenestrata*, abundant in Burmah; first draft.

78. Moths and cocoons of *Attacus Cynthia*, or Ailanthus silkworm.

79. Moths and cocoons of *Attacus Atlas*, North and South India.

80. Moths and cocoons of *Antheræa Yama-mai*.

81. Yarn from cocoons of *Antheræa Yama-mai*.

82. Cloth made from yarn of *Antheræa Yama-mai*, undyed and dyed.

83. Moths and cocoons of *Actias selene*, with drawing of larva.

84. Moths of *Actias leto*.

85. Moths of *Actias mænas*.

86. Large glass case containing Tusser silk cloths printed with native Indian dyestuffs, Indian designs:—

1st side, five specimens.
2nd side, two specimens: palampore and fent.
3rd side, palampore.
4th side, five printed cloths and one hand painted.

Lent by Messrs. Liberty & Co.

87. Case of Tusser silks, illustrative of the various stages in the manufacture, by spinning processes, of Tusser cocoons and waste Tusser silk into yarns and cloths. Prepared and lent by Messrs. Clayton, Marsdens, Holden, & Co., Halifax.

Compartment 1, Tusser raw waste.
" 2, Tusser waste boiled off.
" 3, Tusser waste carded, lap.
" 4, sliver.
" 5, slubbing.
" 6, roving.
" 7, yarns, natural tint 3/2, 5/2, 8/2, 10/2, 15/2, 16/2.
" 8, yarns, natural tint, 20/2, 21/2, 25/2, 30/2, 32/2, 33/2, 35/2, 40/2.

Compartment 9, yarns, dyed.
„ 10, three specimens of figured weaving; Tusser spun cloth.
„ 11, three specimens of figured weaving; Tusser spun cloth.
„ 12, three specimens of figured weaving; Tusser spun cloth.

APPENDIX IV.

DESCRIPTION of the MACHINERY used in Italy and France for reeling cocoons, and the mode of using it.

Cocoon Reeling Machine, made by Messrs. J. Berthaud et Co., Ingénieurs Mécaniciens, Rue de Vendôme, 132, Lyon.

This machine has been drawn on Plates LXIV., LXV., and LXVI., very accurately, to a scale of 1 inch to the foot, in order that it may be reproduced in India should it be found inconvenient to send to Europe for them.

It is in principle and practice the best form of reeling, and that most commonly used in the South of France and Italy. Should its use become general in India, the refinement in the qualities of both mulberry-worm silks and the wild silks would be so marked and bettered that much larger trade would be done. Although vigorous efforts were made by Government in 1831 to improve the reeling of the mulberrry-worm silk of Bengal, and with a large amount of success, the natives seem to have become indifferent, and the qualities of most Bengal silks have fallen from their standard, and are not inquired for in proportion to their deserts if properly reeled. I should indeed be glad if these remarks may have some effect in stimulating the Government, and those in Indian interests in the silk trade, to insist on the European modes of reeling in all silk produced for export. If this were made a condition we should be able to rely more on our own dependencies for silk instead of having to buy such large quantities from China or Japan.

The lettering indicates the same parts of the machine in each drawing:—

A. Cast-iron framework of the reeling machine.

B. Windlass for supplying the motive power; this may be substituted by a pulley for steam power.

C. Driving wheel, cast-iron.

D. Cog-wheel for a motion for the bar P which is to go and come (*de va et vient*), thereby causing the silk to be distributed on the reel instead of its being reeled all in one portion of the reel. Its action is to spread the silk over the reel as it is reeled.

E. Wooden drum wheel on reel axle driven by the friction of the wheel C.

F. Reel on which the silk is wound whilst being drawn off the cocoon, showing silk on its circumference.

G. Bars of reel, one of which is movable to enable the reeler to remove the silk.

H. Lever and ball, which lowers at the will of the reeler, and throws the wooden drum E out of gear instantly stopping the machine.

I. Small cog-wheel driven by D, which see.

J, K, L. Guiding apparatus for placing the silk evenly on the reel.

M. Two bars of glass with brass ornamental triangle at bottom to lead the threads of silk to the reel.

N. Bar of iron with holes and bolts to fasten and steady the machine to a beam or other supporting framework.

O. Continuation of bar, the end of which overhangs the cocoon tray and carries the bar P.

P. Wooden bar containing the croiseur Q and the 2 agate centre guides RR.

Q. Croiseur.

R. Two guides with agate centre, over which the silk passes on its way from the cocoons to the reel.

S. The silk threads on their passage from the cocoon to the reel.

T. Cast-iron frame holding U.

U. Square brass tray holding V and the implements necessary for the reelers' use; namely, vessel for cold water, perforate spatula (Plate LXIII.), small saucepan, brush for "battage" or removing the outside unwindable portion and finding the reelable ends of the silk (Plate LX.)

V. Round tinned copper or pewter basin, 17 ins. diameter and 6 ins. deep, containing the hot water or softening solution in which the cocoons are placed for reeling. This basin has a perforated false bottom through which passes the steam pipe W to heat the contents of the basin. When the heat is supplied with the stove (see Plate LXII., Fig. 2), the pipe is removed by unscrewing the nut at the bottom of the basin and substituting a "champignon" (Plate LXIV., Fig. 1), which serves the purpose of a blank flange.

W. Steampipe.

X. Agate filières in brass frame, through which the filaments pass onwards to the reel forming the thread.

Y. Tray, cup, and pipe in corner of tray to pour off superfluous liquid from any cocoon that requires special attention.

Mode of using the Machinery.

The first operation after purchasing the cocoons is to suffocate them, that is to say, to kill ("étouffir") the chrysalis in the cocoon.

For this operation there are two systems in vogue; the one called "steam killing," the other the "dry killing." As to which of these systems is the better depends on the opinion of the throwster ("filateur"), some preferring the first named, others the second. The apparatus for steam killing consists of a chamber, larger or smaller, into which is introduced a steam jet. The cocoons are spread over trays called cavagues, three or four minutes being sufficient to kill them, the temperature being 70° to 75° (158° to 167° Fahrenheit).

The cocoons having undergone this operation are damp; they are then spread upon the tables, care being taken to move them about from time to time, so that they may dry evenly. Two months are required for the complete drying. As we shall see, the dry operation has not this inconvenience, for the cocoons coming out of it are completely dry and ready to pack. The dry apparatus consists of one large chamber, into which tables with or without wheels ("wagons"), whereon are placed the "caragues" filled with cocoons, are pushed. Two furnaces introduce the hot air which raises the temperature to 70 to 75 degrees. This is hot enough to kill the cocoons in 5 to 6 hours (they may be left in 20 to 22 hours, and then withdrawn perfectly dry). Cocoons having undergone the killing operation are submitted to a further process before being put into winding. This is called the "cocoon sorting." This process is simply, 1st, picking out the dead, the stained, and the double cocoons; 2nd, sorting out the different shades so that the silk may not be streaky; 3rd, sorting the coarser from the fine.

This is a very important operation, being of great assistance to every spinner or winder. As is well known, there is infinite variety in the degrees of coarseness or fineness of the ends, and if not carefully sorted there would be great irregularity in the size. In addition to this, cocoons with coarse ends (called satinés) require much more killing. To produce good silk, these require, 1st, less drying; 2nd, less heating.

If care is not taken in sorting, there would be fine and very coarse ends in the same basin, and some cocoons more dried than others. It would be, as we have already stated, more difficult to reel evenly (or with a regular thread), and in addition to this the silk would be irregular in strength, which would be fatal to one of the chief properties of silk.

The threshing ("battage") of the cocoons is done by means of the "escoubette" or besom by moving this over the cocoons already prepared until their outer covering sticks to it. (This outer covering is termed "frisons.") The thread or end then becomes fine and clear, and constitutes good quality raw. According to the "titre" required, the ends coming from 4, 5, or 6 cocoons are run together. The temperature of the water in the basin should be from 85 to 90 degrees centigrade. Winding too cold causes the silk to lack tenacity.

The cocoons being sorted, put them into the basin (the water should be boiling) to prepare them; an operation which lasts some minutes, and of which the duration varies according to the nature of the cocoons. The cocoons being prepared and cleared,—that is, threshed with the besoms in such a manner that the fibre of the cocoons remains attached to it,—all the ends from the cocoons are attached together to the frisons-hook, which is found in front of the platétage; you then detach 8 or 10 cocoons and join the threads together by fours or fives, and pass each of these united threads (*i.e.*, four or five ends put together) into the two ends of the drawplate, or of the drawplate carrier, to the hinge F, placed at the back of the basin. You then lay these two threads across together by means of the "croiseur" H, attaching the two ends of the fork of the said "croiseur." The two ends are then separated in coming from the "croiseur," and are each passed to one of the end carriers G, passing them on each side of the guider placed at the règle E, so that they may be only twisted one half turn in front of the guider, so that if one of the threads should break, the other remaining comes out of the blade of the "asple" to go winding itself up on the shaft. This operation accomplished, the "asple" is turned until a break-down occurs, in which case the winder stops the "asple" or "tour" (wheel) by means of the throw-off D. This "débarquage" D may be worked by the foot.

When several of the cocoons are broken or finished, the winder must at once replace them, taking from those that are attached to the "frisons" (button), and throwing with the end of the forefinger under the "filière" at the top of the basin, so that those ends attach themselves to the remaining thread. The regularity of the "titres" of the silk depends entirely on the regularity with which the thread winding is fed by at once replacing with fresh cocoons any broken down or run out. The "titre" of the silk is found by winding 400 turns of silk on the gauge, or 476 métres, and weighing these 476 métres with the small weights, called deniers, supplied with the balance.

Good cocoons will sustain a strong "croiseur." Inferior will only sustain a relatively weak one.

APPENDIX V.

Lyons' Chambers of Commerce and Wild Silks.

In 1880, at the request of Monsieur Rondot, president of the jury, class 34 (silks), at the Paris Exhibition of 1878, and member of the Lyons Chamber of Commerce, and of several other influential gentlemen connected with the silk industry of France, I had the honour to send to the Chamber of Commerce, Lyons, a collection similar to that exhibited by the Government of India at the Paris Exhibition of 1878.

A copy of the letter acknowledging this gift is appended, together with a translation of an extract from the proceedings of the Lyons Chamber of Commerce giving the results of certain experiments on the Indian silks.

La Chambre de Commerce de Lyon à Monsieur Thomas Wardle.

Monsieur, Lyon, le 18 Mai 1880.

Vous avez bien voulu faire don à notre Chambre de Commerce d'une collection très complète et très intéressante de papillons, cocons, soies grèges et ouvrées, soies teintes, et tissus unis et façonnés, provenant de diverses espèces de vers à soie qui, dans l'Inde, se nourrissent de feuilles autres que celles du mûrier.

Nous ne saurions vous exprimer, monsieur, combien notre chambre a été sensible à cette libéralité hors ligne. Elle comprend que ce n'est pas sans beaucoup d'efforts et de récherches qu'une telle collection a pu être réunie. Les catalogues et informations méthodiques qui l'accompagnaient, en la rendant encore plus précieuse à nous, ont fait apprécier l'esprit tout à la fois scientifique et pratique qui vous avait guidé.

C'est un fait désormais acquis, ce nous semble, d'une part, qu'il est possible de tirer de ces cocons sauvages des soies d'une finesse relativement grande; et d'autre part, que ces matières, traitées par des procédés qui sont en partie votre œuvre, sont susceptibles de recevoir une diversité de teintes et de nuances de nature à satisfaire à toutes les exigences des consommations.

A ce point de vue, la collection que nos industriels seront appelés à étudier leur ouvrira sans doute une nouvelle source de travail; et c'est là, monsieur, ce qui distingue votre libéralité des dons plus ou moins recommandables qui sont faits quelque fois à notre musée. Aussi, notre chambre a-t-elle pris soin de la signaler à M. le Ministre de l'Agriculture et du Commerce, par une lettre spéciale; et elle a donné des ordres pour qu'une vitrine lui fût attribuée dans son musée, avec mention du nom du donateur.

Nous vous prions, Monsieur, d'agréer, avec l'expression de notre gratitude, l'assurance de notre considération la plus distinguée.

Le President,
(Signé) Oscar Galline.

Le Secrétaire,
(Signé) F. A. Severn.

Extract from the Minutes of the Proceedings of the Chamber of Commerce of Lyons,

At the Meeting of the 17th February 1881.

Present:

Mons. Sevène, Vice-President,
MM. de la Rochette, Roche-Alix, Osmont, Fougasse, Mulaton, Marius Duc, McRoe, Payen, Desgeorges, Paule, Pariscot, and
Gourd, Secretary.

M. Sevène, the Vice-President, presented the following report:—

Messieurs,

It is within the recollection of the Chamber that, in the month of January 1879, the Indian Government sent to the Chamber, at Mr. N. Rondot's request, two cases of Eria and Mooga cocoons, with the request that they might be experimented upon in France. These cases contained smothered and bitten cocoons. The Chamber has only received during the last few days the reports drawn up by the manufacturers to whom we have submitted the cocoons.

The spinning cocoons have been divided in two lots, and confided to two manufacturers. The yield, after immersion, varied between 8 and 9 kilogrammes, that is to say, that 8 or 9 kilogrammes of cocoons were necessary to obtain a kilogramme of silk, whilst 4 to 4½ kilogrammes of *Bombyx du mûrier* (*Bombyx mori*) are sufficient. This small proportion is due to this circumstance, that the outside shell of the cocoon has to be removed before the good silk is reached, and the quantity of silk to be reeled is diminished by so much.

The expense of spinning would be about 10 francs per kilogramme.

The raw silk appears to be very light; therefore the loss in scouring would not be considerable.

A most careful sorting ("triage rigoureux") of the cocoons is the first condition to be fulfilled in order to facilitate the spinning, which would require special care. This is a point on which the two manufacturers to whom we have confided the cocoons rightly insist, and upon which it seems to us the attention of the Indian Government must be particularly called.

The same observation was made to us by Messieurs Franck perè et fils and Martelin, who have consented to make experiments on the lot of bitten cocoons.

In order to give a chance of success to the importation of these cocoons, they say in their report:—

"The first condition would be to insist on a most careful sorting, by the shippers, of the light and dark cocoons. The latter should be rejected; we consider them useless on account of their colour. The strongest scouring is not sufficient to bleach them enough for the consumers of *schappes* (waste silk thread) to use regularly the thread thus obtained.

"On the other hand, there is no objection to the regular use of the light cocoons.

"The experiment we have made has been satisfactory enough.

"In the scouring we have had to lose about 3 per cent. more than with the ordinary cocoons, in order to obtain a material well prepared for combing. Notwithstanding this, and although the cocoons are comparatively light in colour, this material has retained a terreous tint rather objectionable, which leads us to fear that some difficulty might be met with when dyeing certain shades.

"In the combing we have obtained the usual yield.

"The threads are long and shiny, in spite of their little fineness due to the origin of the cocoons, and their elasticity ("souplesse") is sufficient to allow of their being easy to spin.

"The price of cocoons being most variable, it is not possible to state the value of these cocoons.

"We think that this value must be about 30 °/₀ (thirty per cent.) below that of the silk-worm house cocoons. That difference is accounted for by the loss in scouring, the colour of the material and its want of fineness.

"Good European seed, yielding about 80 °/₀ of silky matter for working into silk and 20 °/₀ chrysalis and other waste, is worth on an average 10 francs.

"Good light Tussah cocoons, yielding about the same quantity of silky matter, would almost surely find buyers at 30 °/₀ less, say 7 francs.

"Large quantities of Japanese cocoons are brought to Marseilles, and sold at prices not exceeding 2 or 3 francs; the price of 7 francs must be amply remunerative to make it advantageous to send such cocoons to Europe."

It results from this report that the importation of bitten Tussah cocoons is very likely to prove successful. The threads obtained by Messieurs Franck père et fils and Martelin are very fine, and would surely be used in the manufacture of mixed fabrics, silk and schappes, and cotton and schappes (waste silk threads).

The importation of smothered cocoons might perhaps be less advantageous; the Indians have a superiority over us on account of the low price of labour, which enables them to reel the silk very slowly and to turn it to the best possible account.

The value of the cocoons appears to us to be too low to incur considerable expenses of shipping, on account of the size and weight of the cocoons, of which the chrysalis forms a by no means inconsiderable part.

Such is, messieurs, the answer I propose to give to the

Indian Government, together with our thanks for having sent the cocoons and submitted them to our examination.

This report having been read,

The Chamber decided that it should be sent to the Minister of Agriculture and Commerce, with a request that it might be forwarded to the Indian Minister in London.

Samples of the threads obtained both from the smothered and bitten cocoons to be annexed to this report.

This extract certified correct by
Le Secrétaire, Membre de la Chambre,
(Signed) A. GOURD.

Seal
of the Chamber of Commerce
of Lyons.

INDEX.

PLATE I.

FIG. 1.

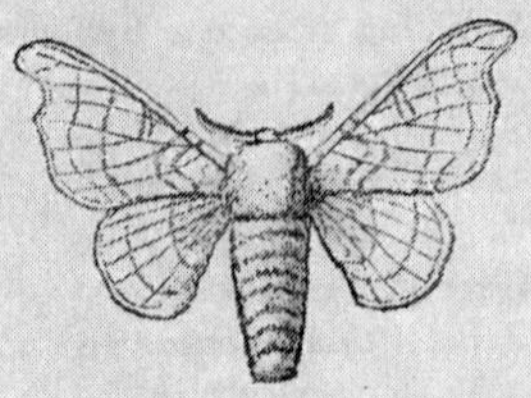

Bombyx mori, or mulberry feeding silkworm (Male).

FIG. 2.

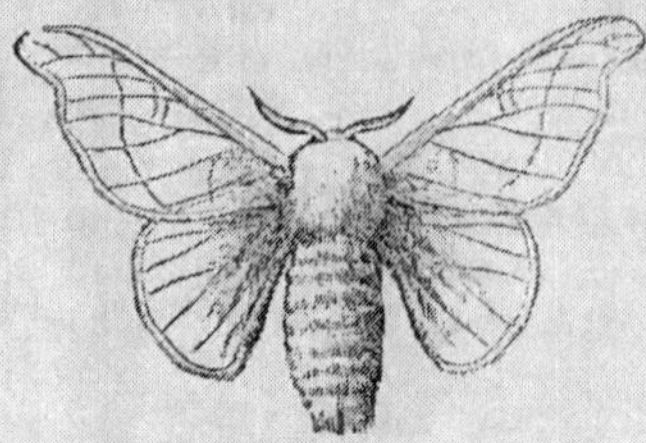

Bombyx mori (Female).

FIG. 3.

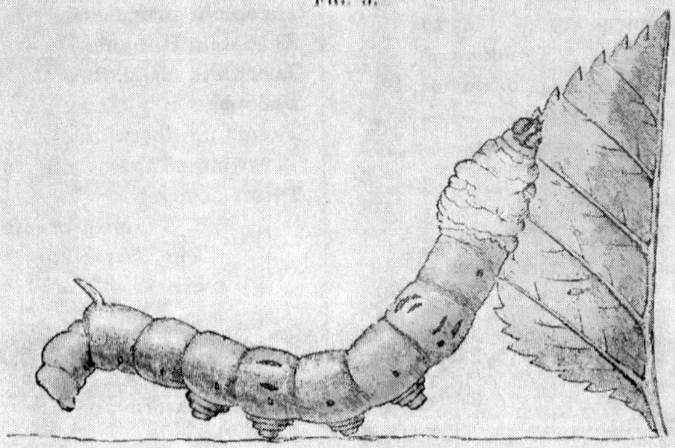

Larva of Bombyx mori.

FIG. 4.

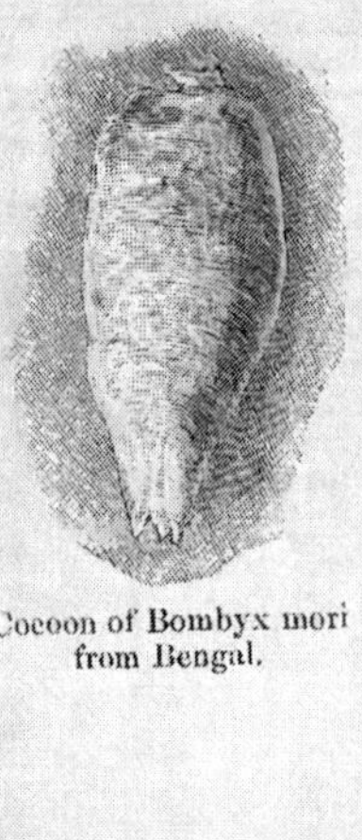

Cocoon of Bombyx mori from Bengal.

FIG. 5.

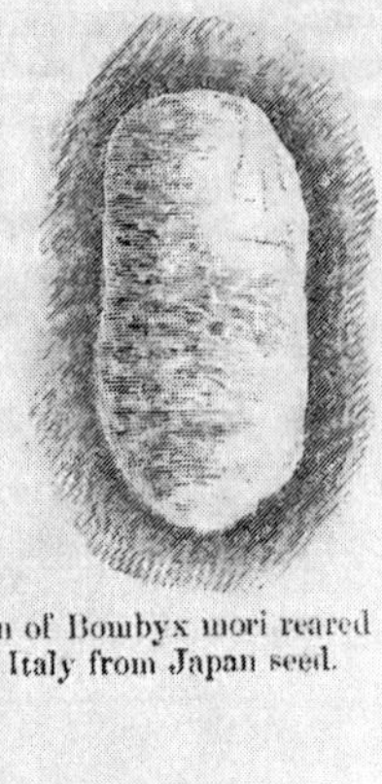

Cocoon of Bombyx mori reared in Italy from Japan seed.

PLATE II.

FIG. 1.

Antheræa mylitta or Tusser moth (Male).

FIG. 3.

Antheræa mylitta or Tusser moth (Female).

PLATE III.

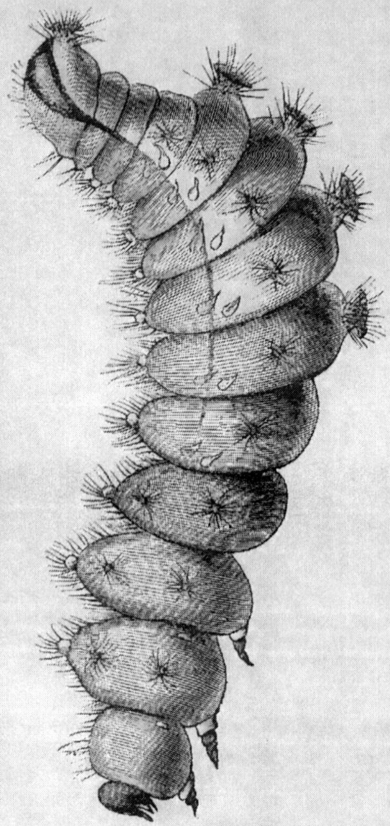

Larva of Antheræa mylitta or Tusser silkworm.

PLATE IV.

FIG. 1.

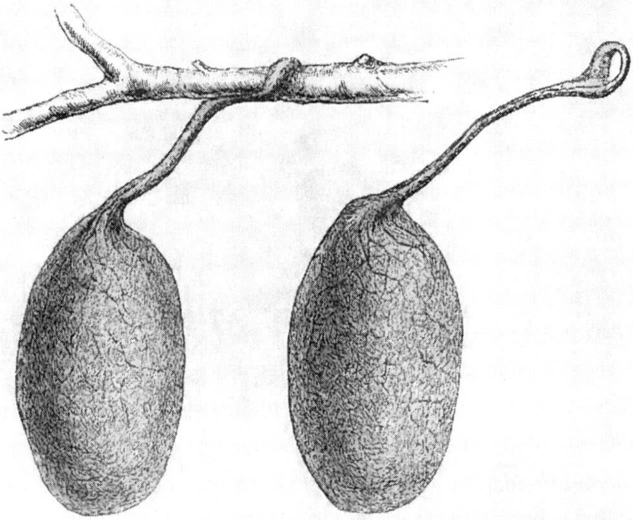

Tusser cocoons.

FIG. 2.

Tusser cocoon cut open to show the chrysalis inside.

PLATE V.

FIG. 1.

Antheræa Assama or Muga moth (Male).

FIG. 2.

Antheræa Assama or Muga moth (Female).

PLATE VI

FIG. 1.

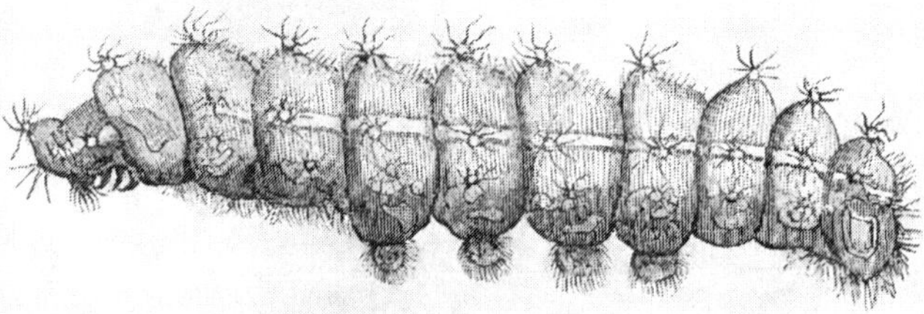

Larva of Antheræa Assama or Muga silkworm.

FIG. 2.

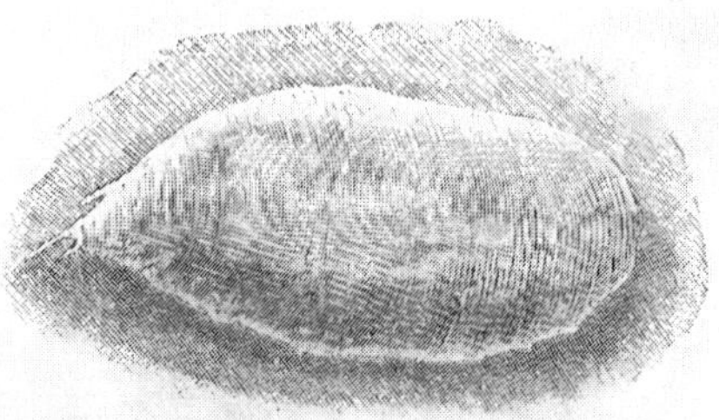

Muga cocoon.

PLATE VII.

Fig. 1.

Antheræa Roylei (Female).

Fig. 2.

Antheræa Frithii (Male).

PLATE VIII.

FIG. 1.

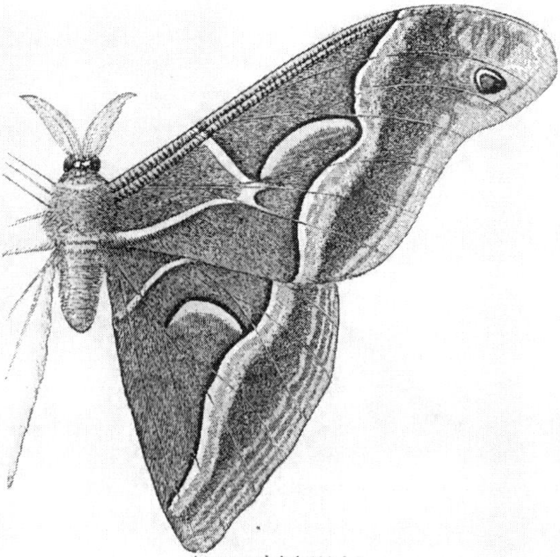

Attacus ricini (Male).

FIG. 2.

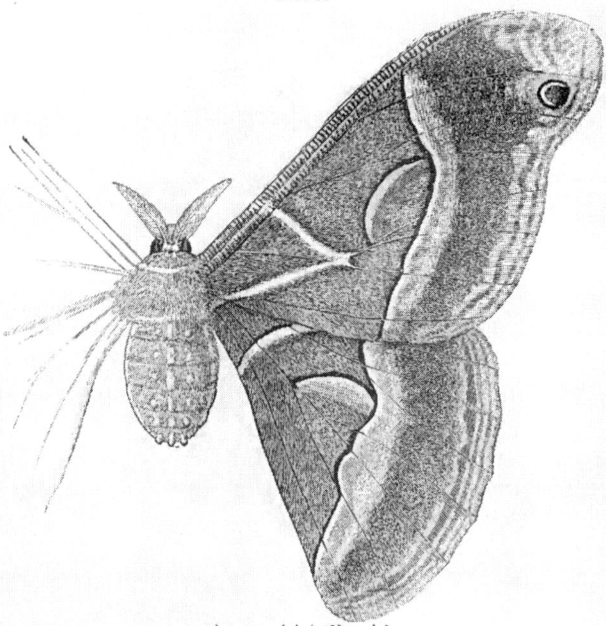

Attacus ricini (Female).

PLATE IX

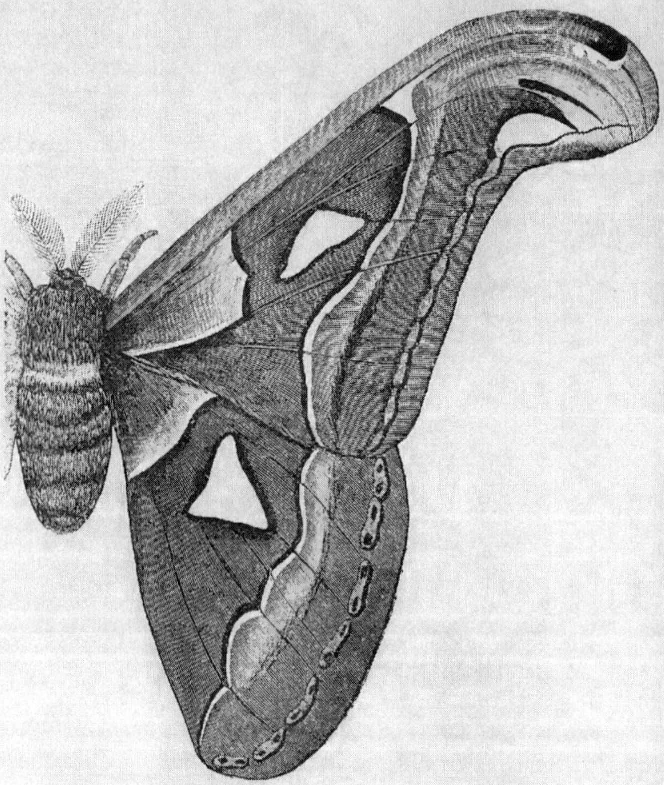

Attacus Atlas (Male).

PLATE X.

Attacus Atlas (Female).

PLATE XI.

FIG. 1.

Larva of Attacus Atlas or Atlas silkworm.

FIG. 2.

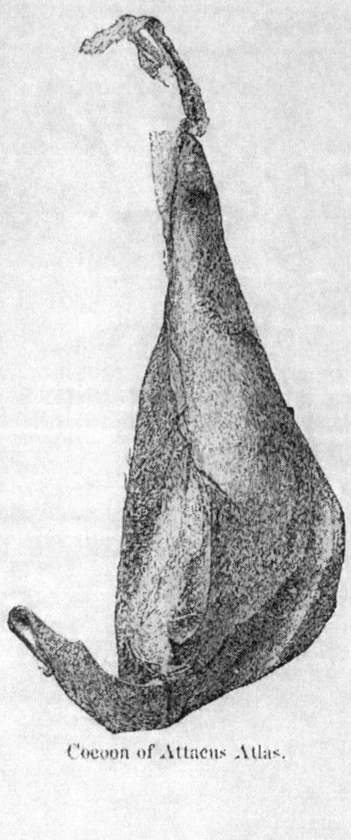

Cocoon of Attacus Atlas.

PLATE XII.

FIG. 1.

Cricula trifenestrata (Male).

FIG. 2.

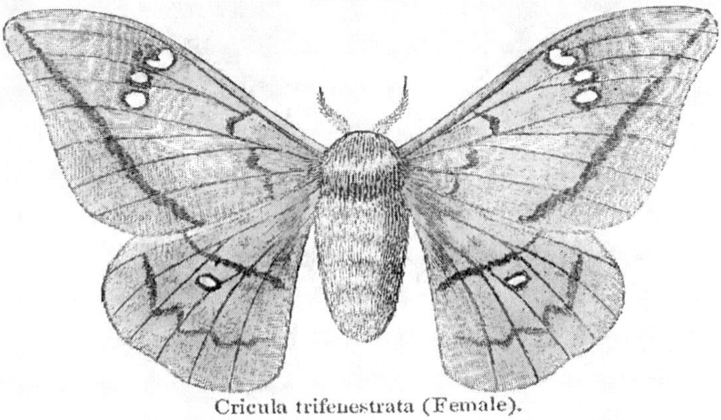

Cricula trifenestrata (Female).

FIG. 3.

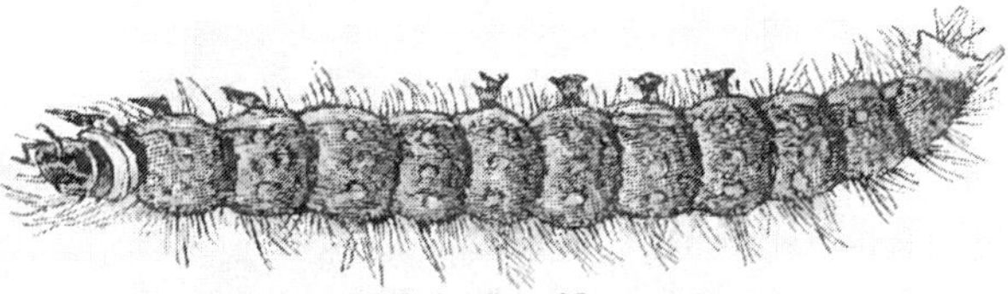

Larva of Cricula trifenestrata.

FIG. 4.

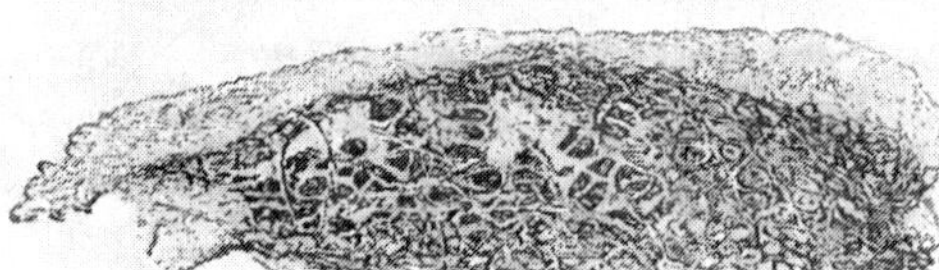

Cocoon of Cricula trifenestrata.

PLATE XIII.

FIG. 1.

Actias selene (Male).

FIG. 2.

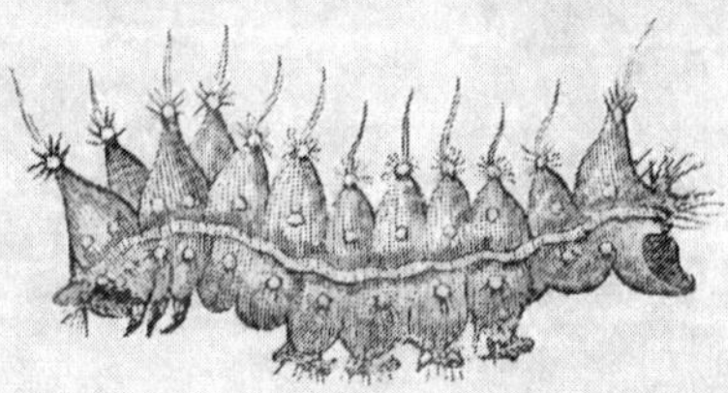

Larva of Actias selene.

FIG. 3.

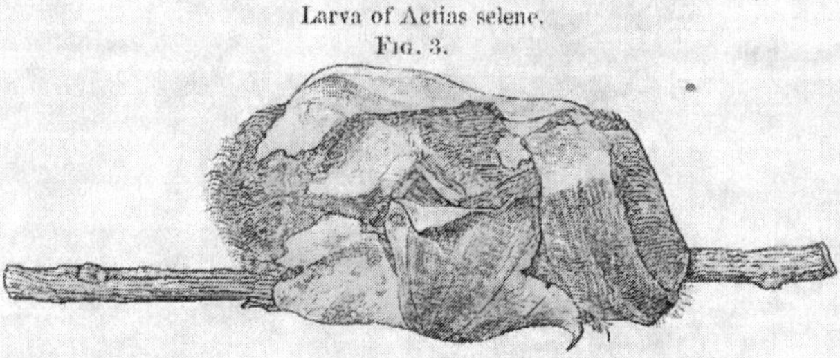

Cocoon of Selene.

PLATE XIV.

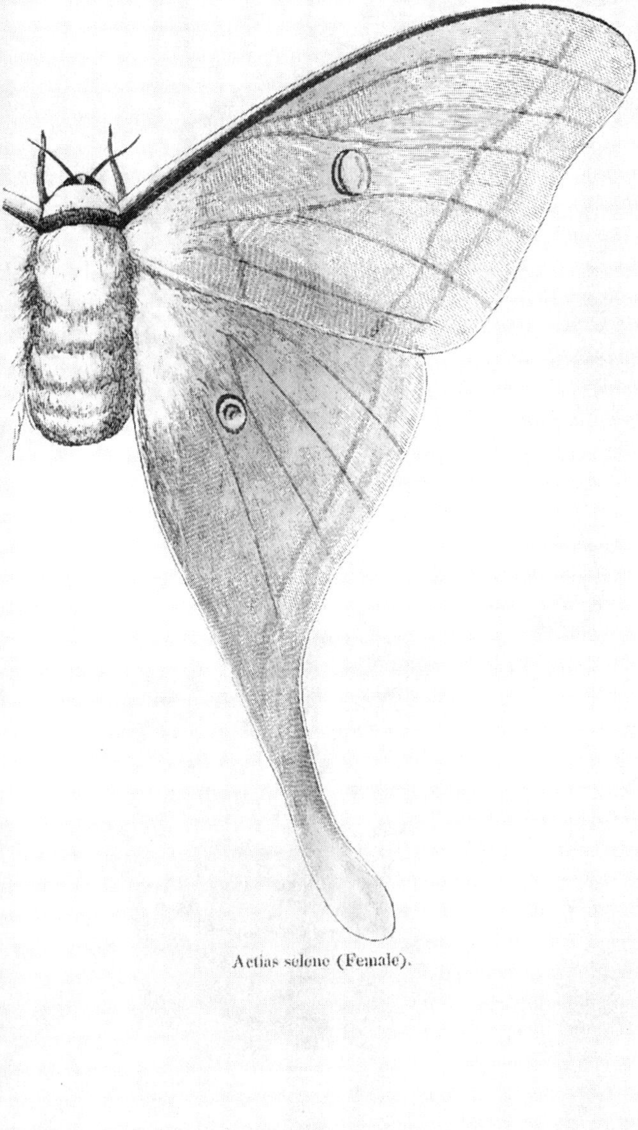

Actias selene (Female).

PLATE XV.

Fig. 1.

Antheræa Helferi (Male).

Fig. 2.

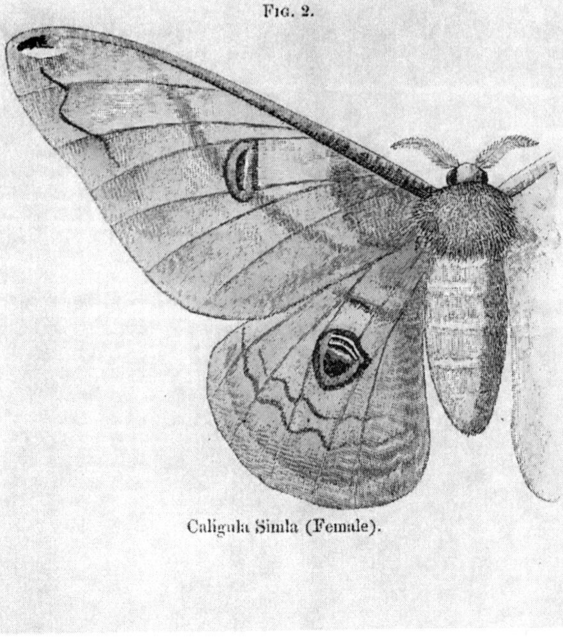

Caligula Simla (Female).

PLATE XVI.

FIG. 1.

Antheræa pernyi (Male).

FIG. 2.

Antheræa pernyi (Female).

FIG. 3.

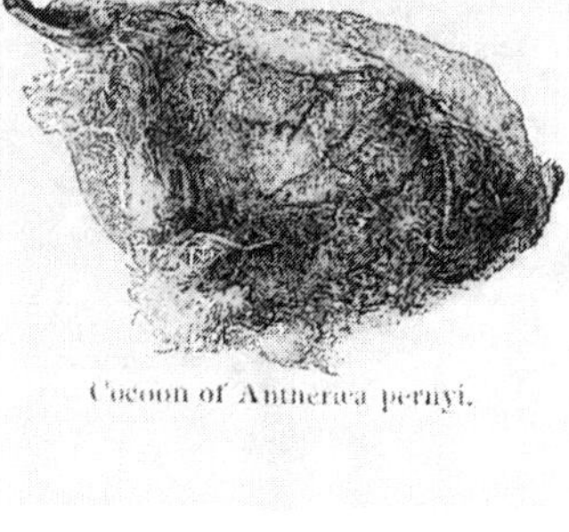

Cocoon of Antheræa pernyi.

PLATE XVII

FIG. 1.

Antheræa yama-mai (Male).

FIG. 2.

Antheræa yama-mai (Female)

PLATE XVIII.

FIG. 1.

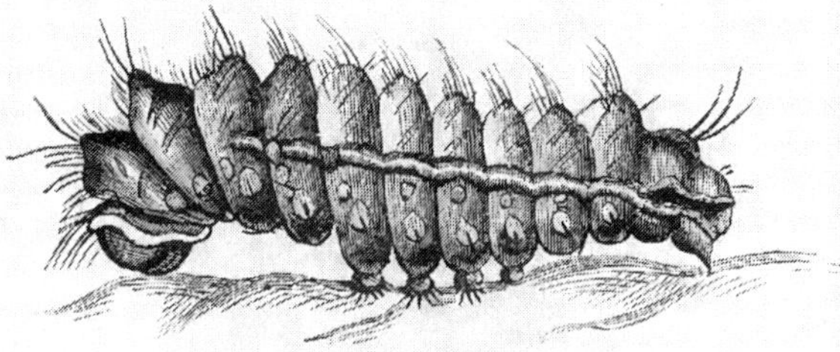

Larva of Antheræa yama-mai.

FIG. 2.

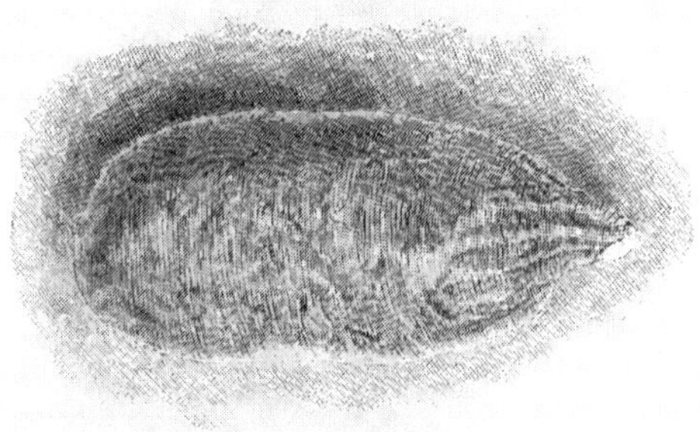

Cocoon of Antheræa yama-mai.

FIG. 3.

Cocoon of Attacus ricini.

PLATE XIX.

FIG. 1.

Attacus cynthia (Male).

FIG. 2.

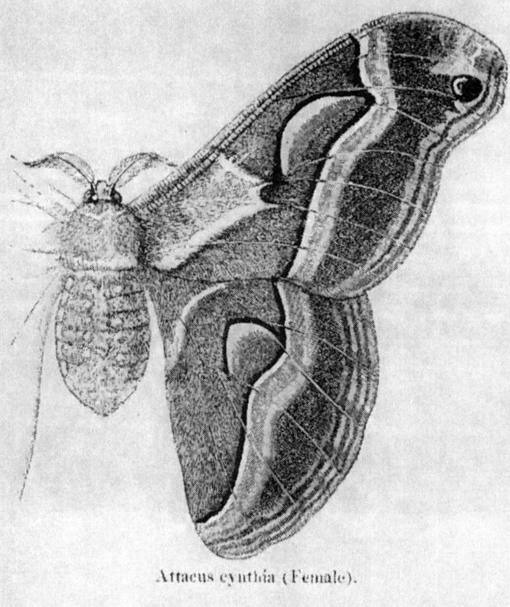

Attacus cynthia (Female).

PLATE XX.

FIG. 1.

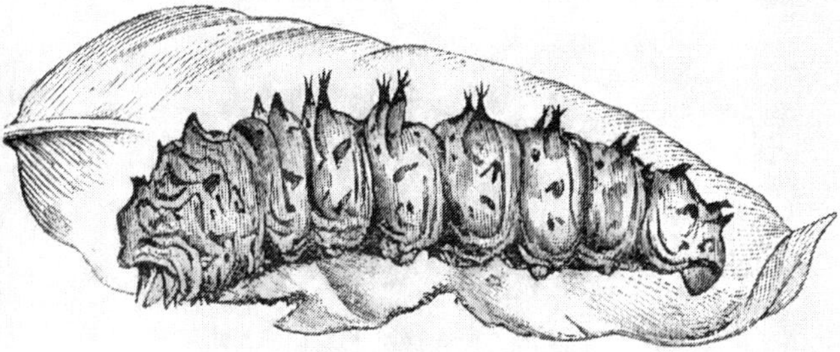

Larva of Attacus cynthia.

FIG. 2.

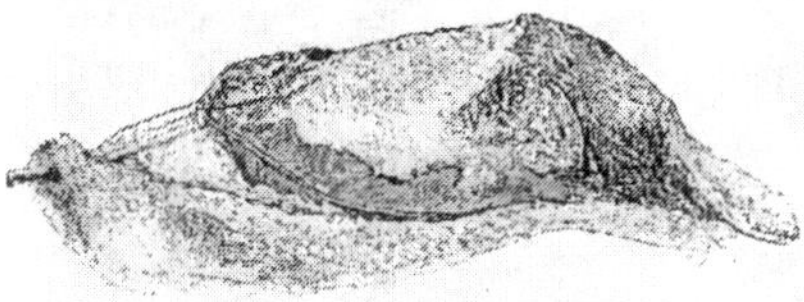

Cocoon of Attacus cynthia.

FIG. 3.

Neoris Huttoni.

PLATE XXI.

FIG. 1.

Saturnia carpini (Male).

FIG. 2.

Saturnia carpini (Female).

FIG. 3.

Saturnia Grotei (Female).

PLATE XXII.

FIG. 1.

Loepa katinka (Male).

FIG. 2.

Loepa katinka (Female).

FIG. 3.

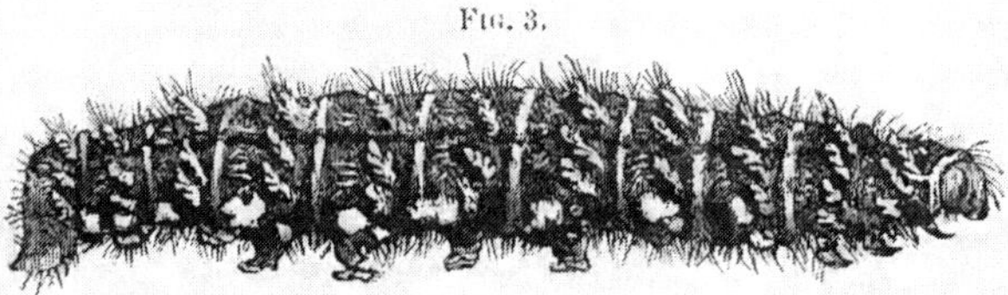

Larva of Loepa katinka.

PLATE XXIII.

FIG. 1.

Loepa miranda (Male).

FIG. 2.

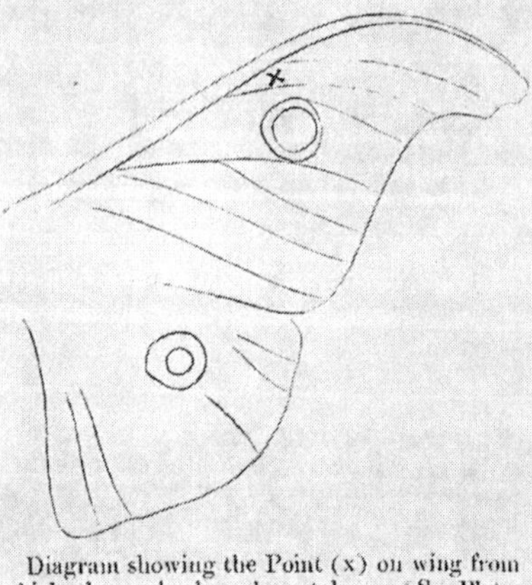

Diagram showing the Point (x) on wing from which the scales have been taken. (*See* Plates XLIX to LIV.)

PLATE XXIV.

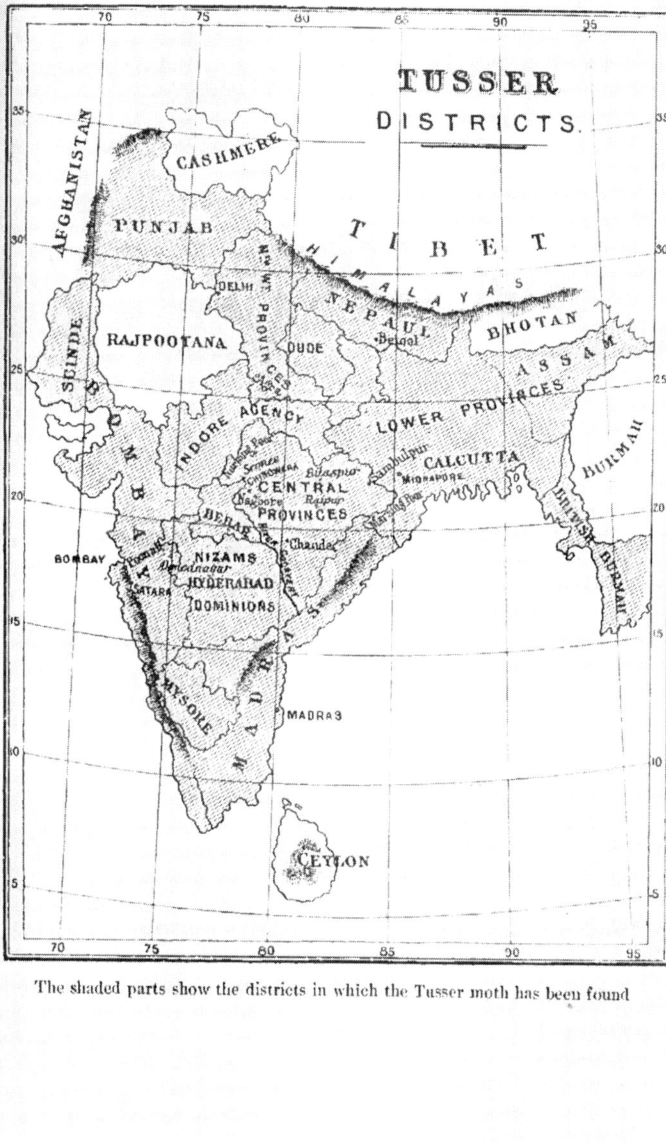

The shaded parts show the districts in which the Tusser moth has been found

PLATE XXV.

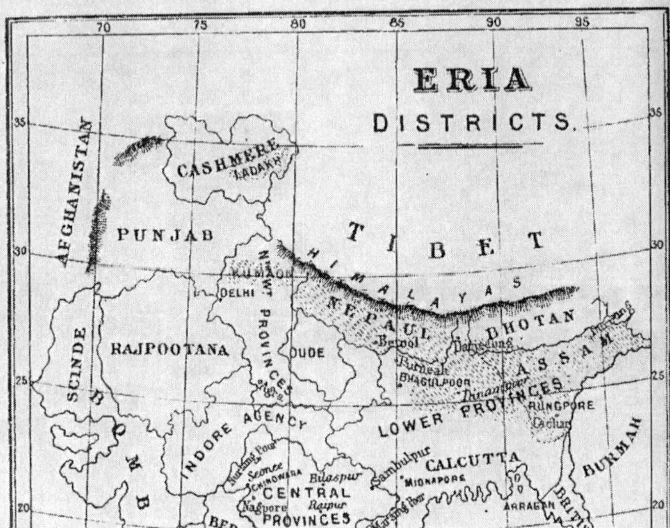

The shaded parts show the districts in which the Eria moth (*Attacus ricini*) has been found.

PLATE XXVI.

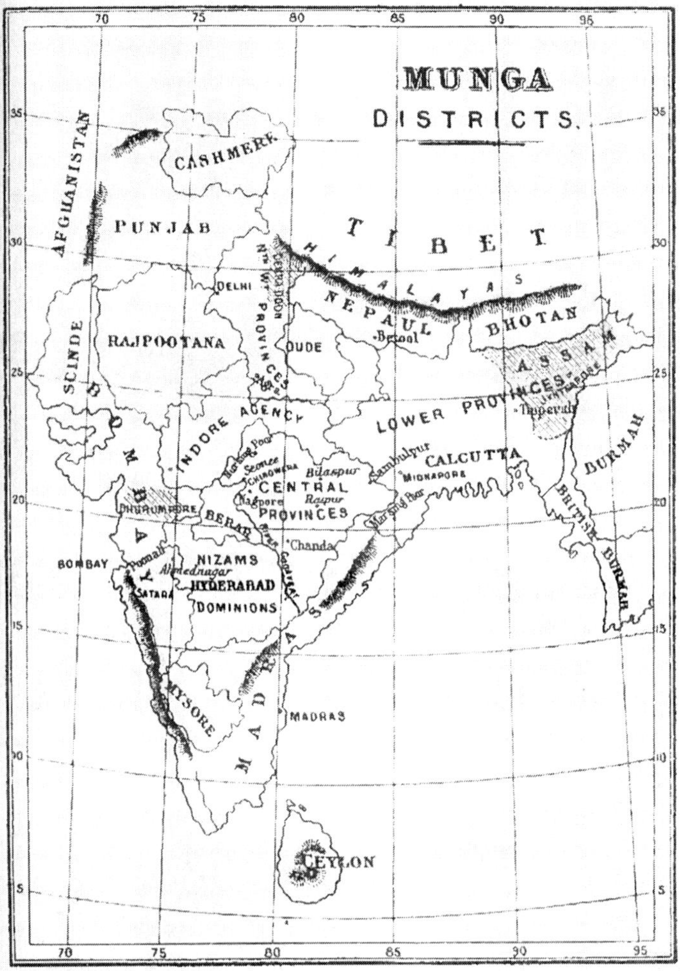

The shaded parts show the districts in which the Munga or Muga moth (*Autheræa Assama*) has been found.

PLATE XXVII.

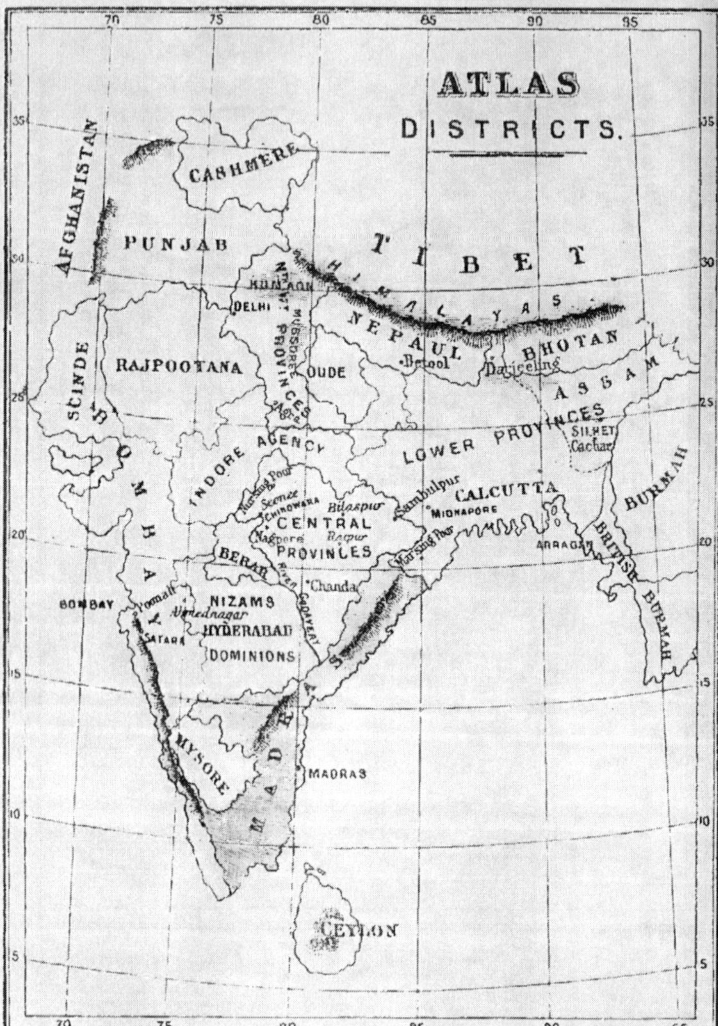

The shaded parts show the districts in which the Atlas moth has been found.

PLATE XXVIII.

FIG. 1.

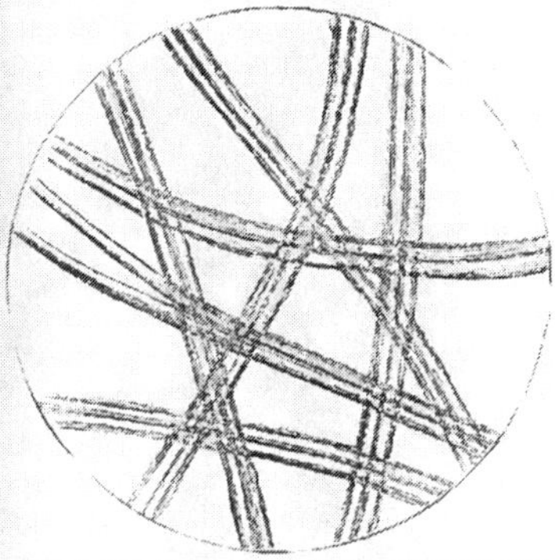

Silk of Bombyx mori, or silk of commerce.

FIG. 2.

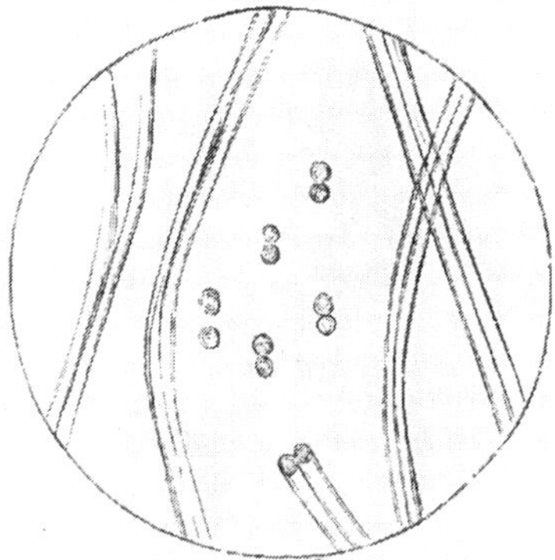

Silk of Bombyx mori, showing transverse sections.

FIG. 3.

Silk of Antheræa mylitta or Tusser silk.

FIG. 4.

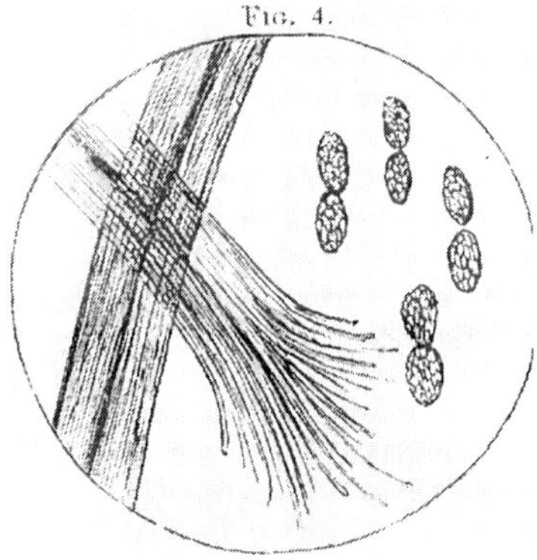

Silk of Antheræa mylitta or Tusser silk, showing fibrets and transverse sections.

FIG. 5.

Silk of Antheræa Assama or Muga silk.

FIG. 6.

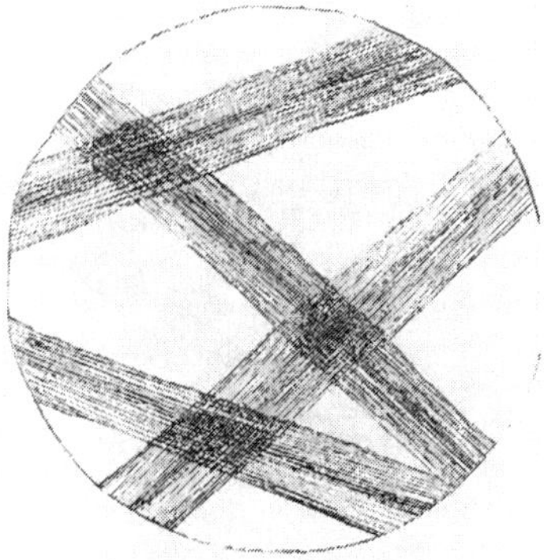

Silk of Antheræa pernyi.

PLATE XXIX.

Fig. 1.

Silk of Actias selene.

Fig. 2.

Silk of Attacus ricini or Eria silk.

Fig. 3.

Silk of Attacus Atlas.

Fig. 4.

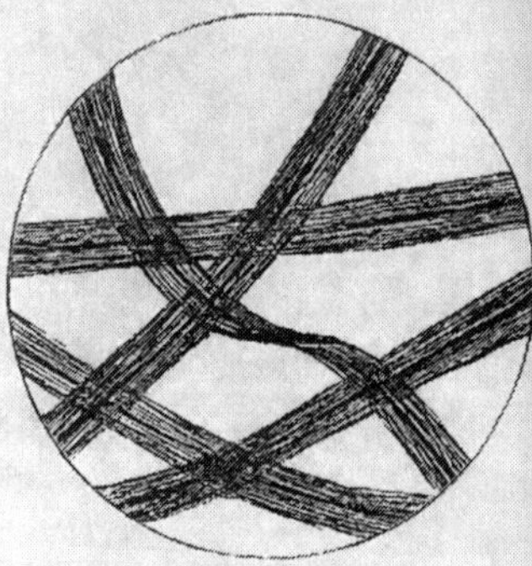

Silk of Cricula trifenestrata.

Fig. 5.

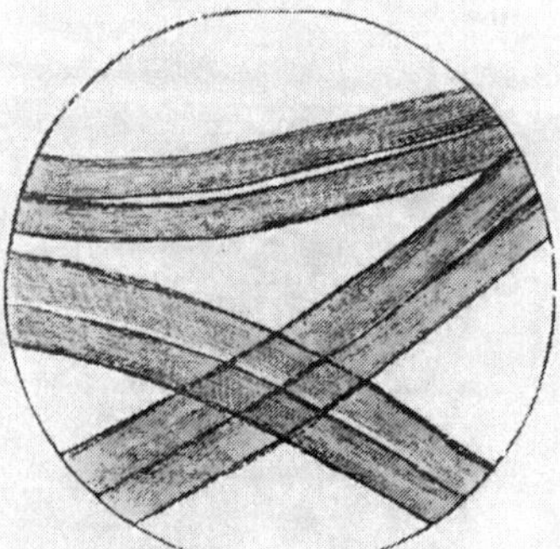

Silk of Antheræa yama-mai.

Fig. 6.

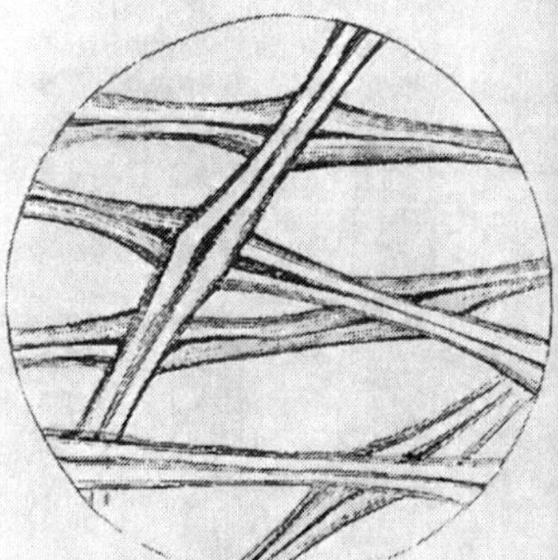

Silk of Saturnia carpini.

PLATE XXX.

Tectona grandis.

PLATE XXXI.

Terminalia Catappa.

PLATE XXXII.

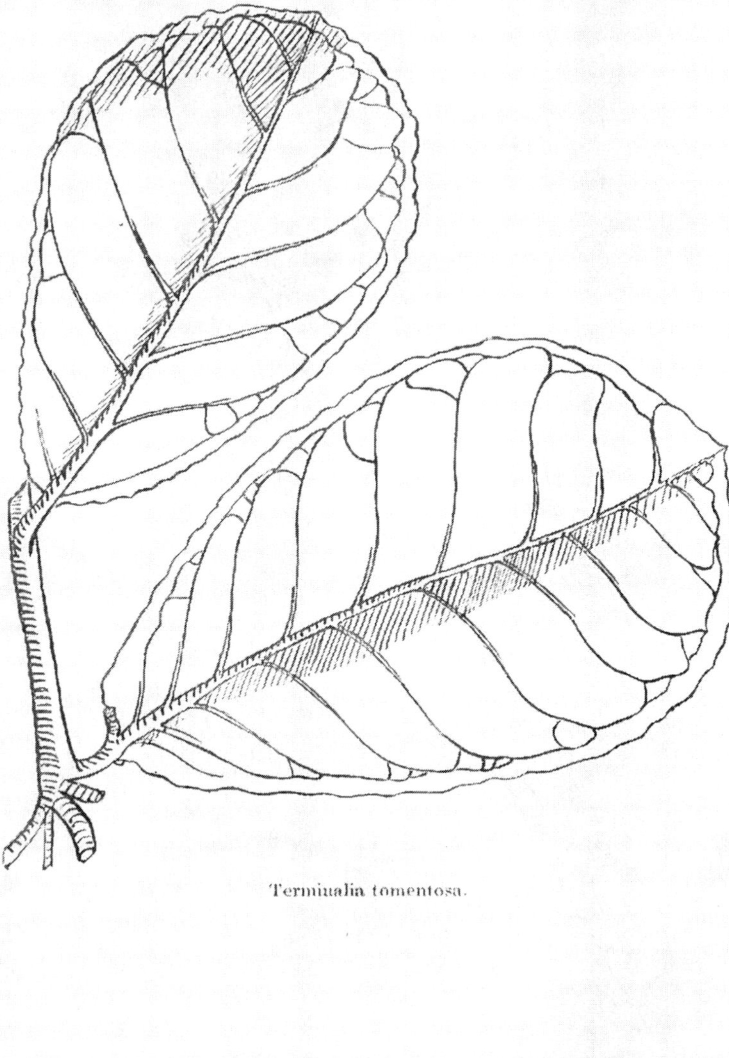

Terminalia tomentosa.

PLATE XXXIII.

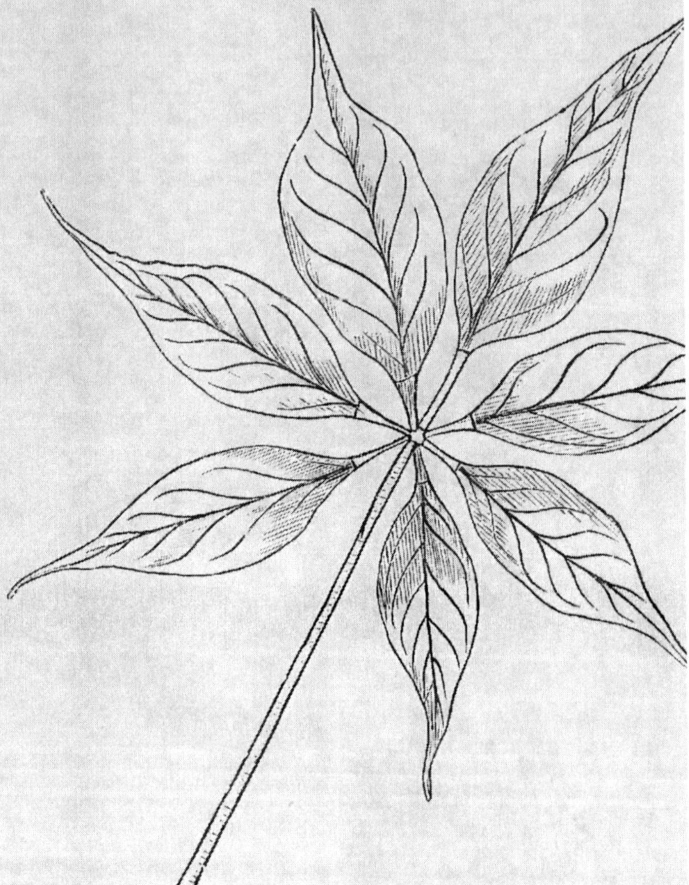

Bombax heptaphyllum.

PLATE XXXIV.

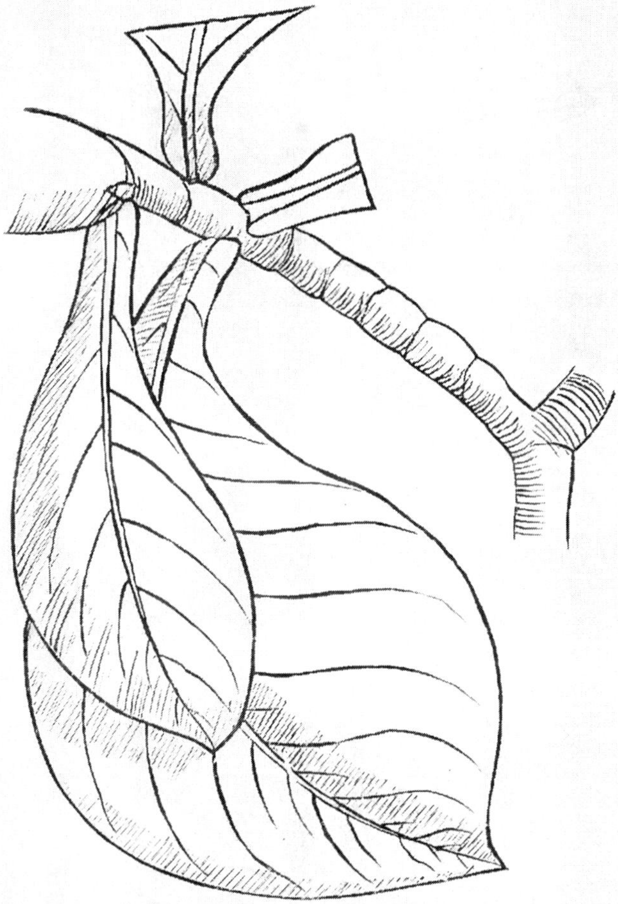

Careya sphærica.

PLATE XXXV.

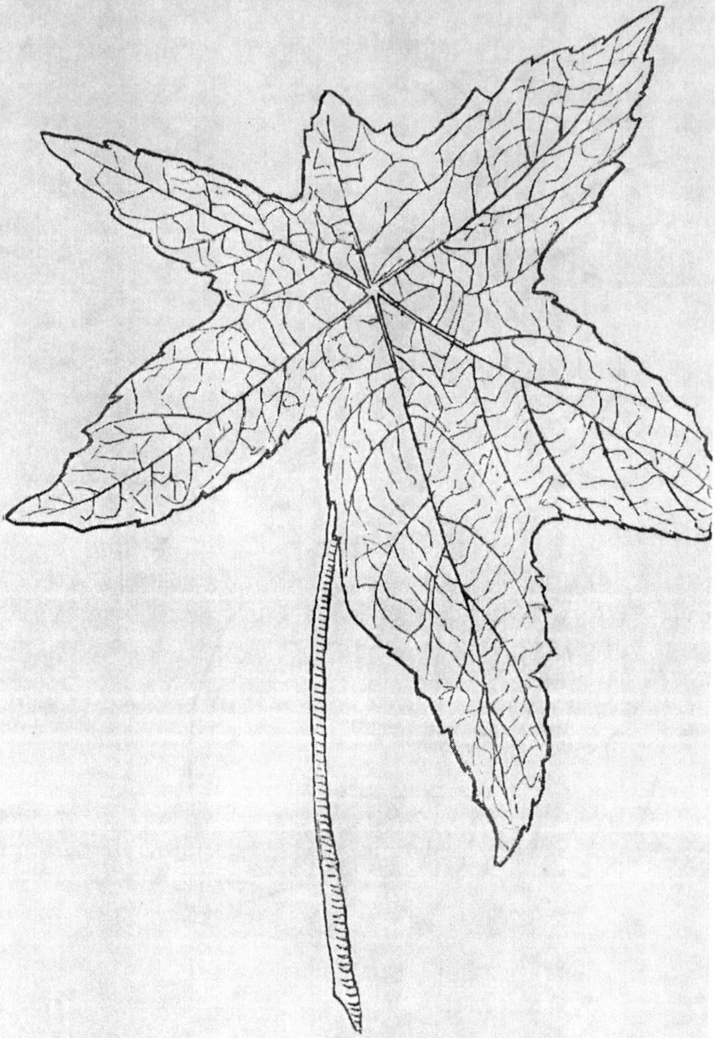

Ricinus communis.

PLATE XXXVI.

Lagerstræmia Indica

PLATE XXXVII.

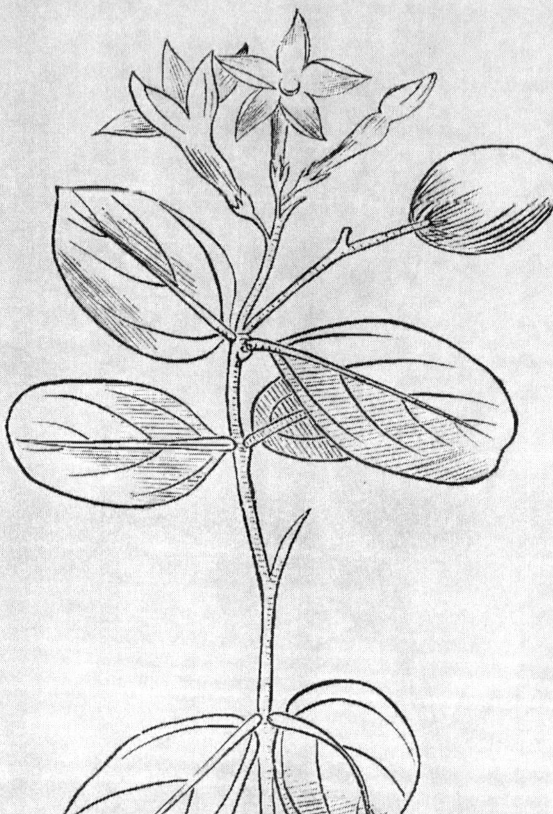

Carissa Carandas.

PLATE XXXVIII.

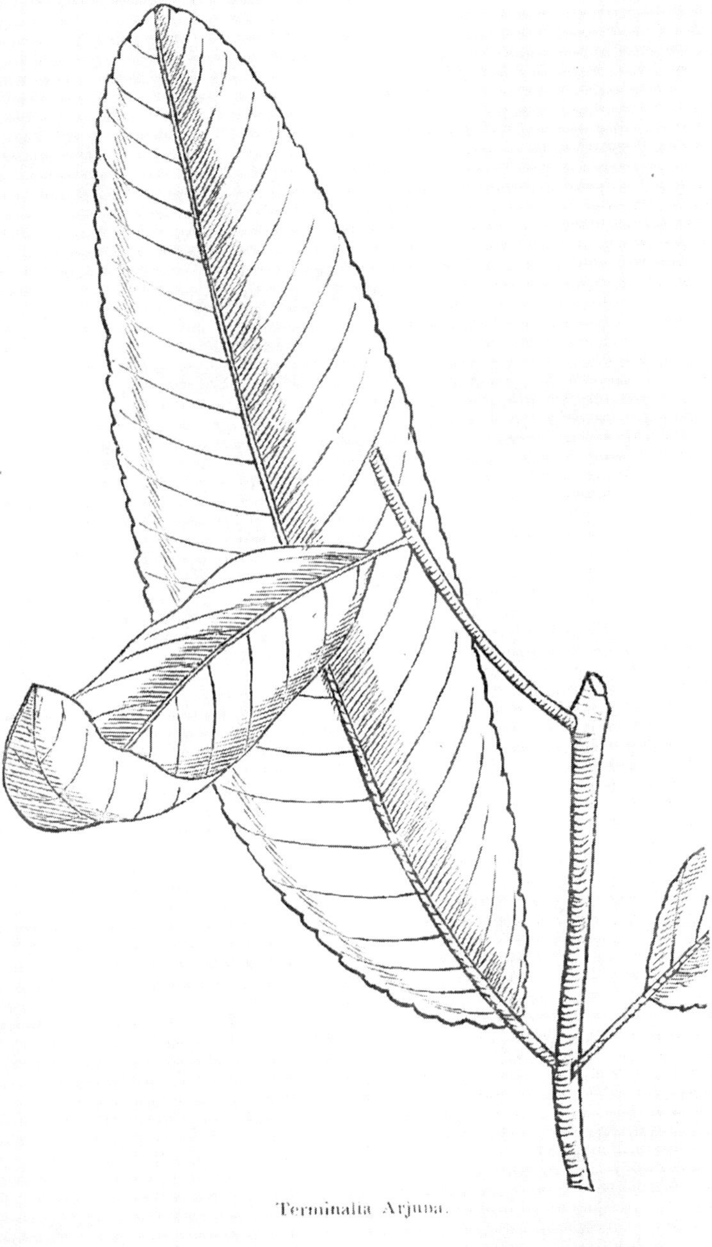

Terminalia Arjuna.

PLATE XXXIX.

Ficus Benjaminia

PLATE XL.

Morus alba (the Mulberry).

PLATE XLI.

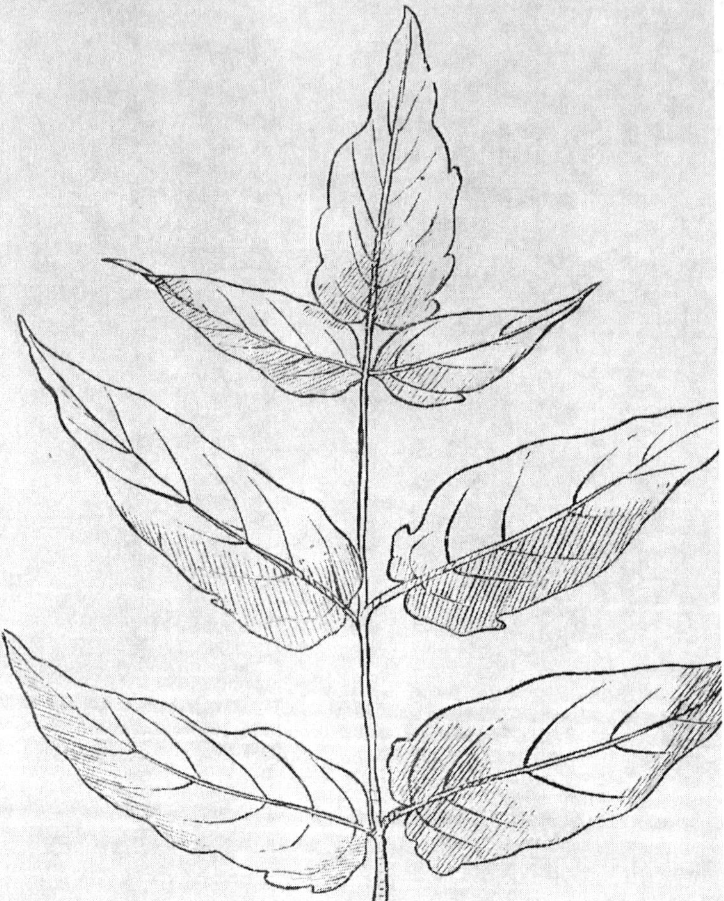

Ailanthus glandulosa.

PLATE XLII.

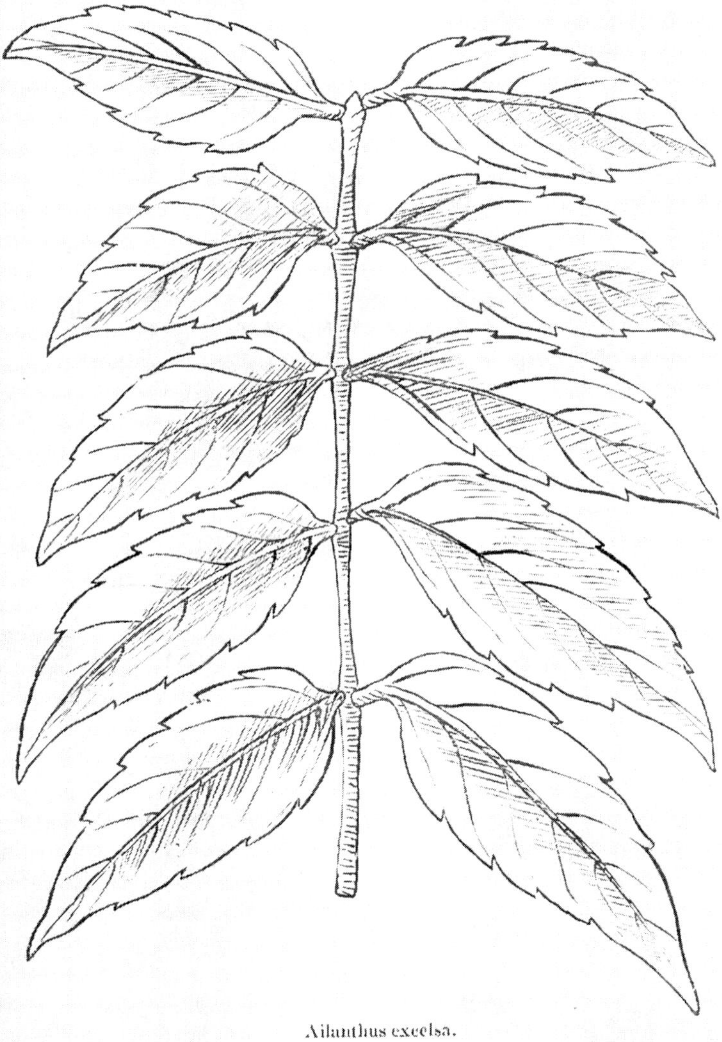

Ailanthus excelsa.

PLATE XLIII.

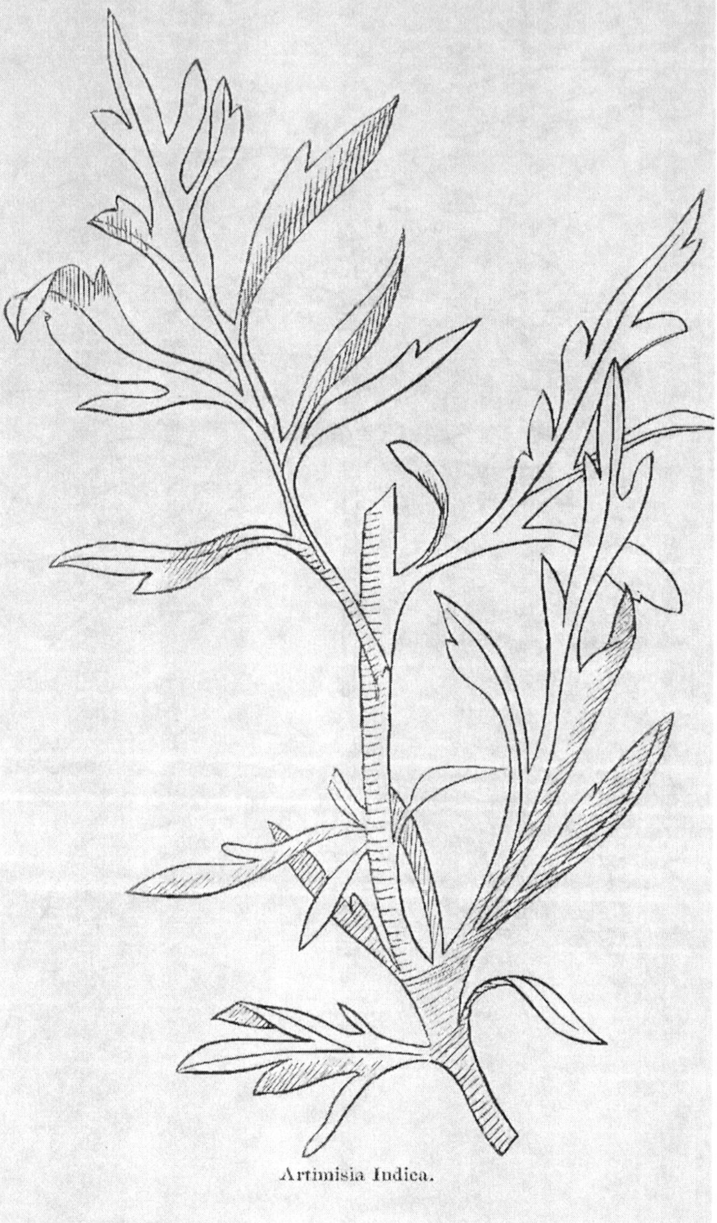

Artimisia Indica.

PLATE XLIV.

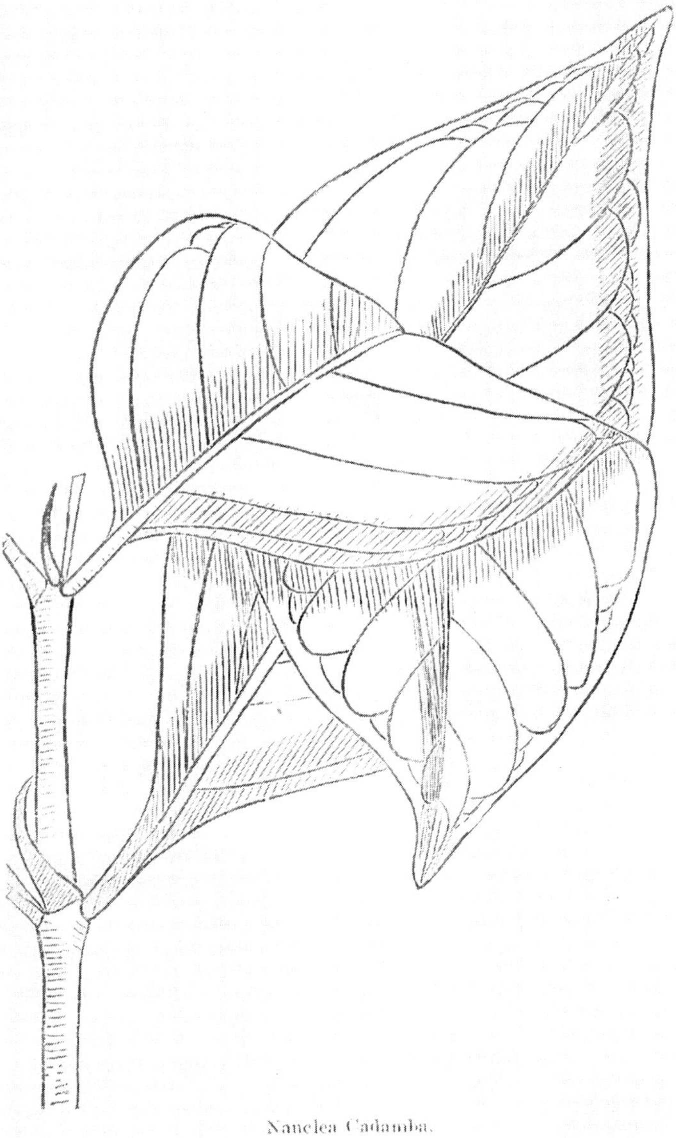

Nauclea Cadamba.

PLATE XLV.

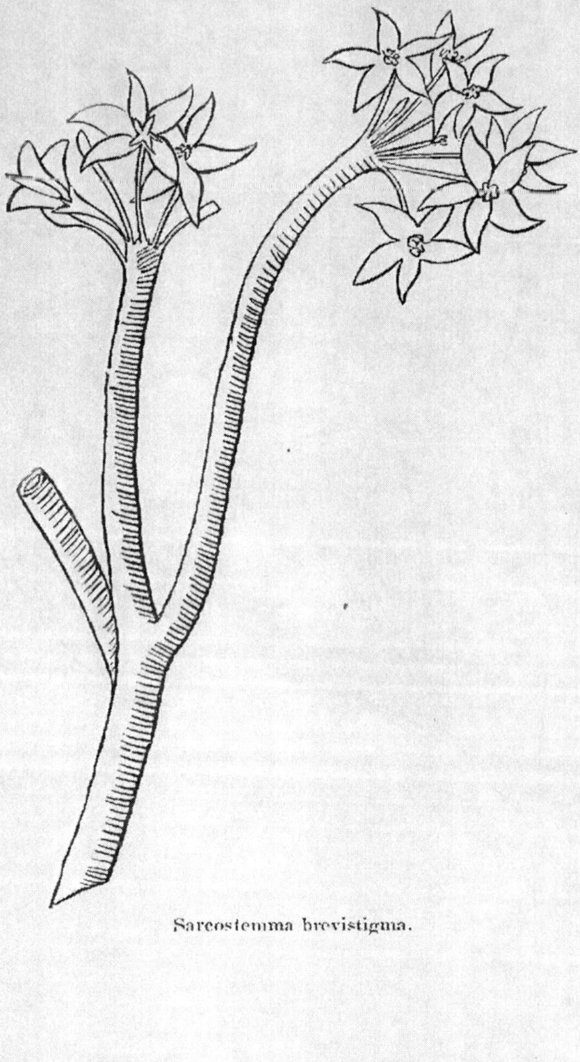

Sarcostemma brevistigma.

PLATE XLVI.

Coriaria nipalensis.

PLATE XLVII.

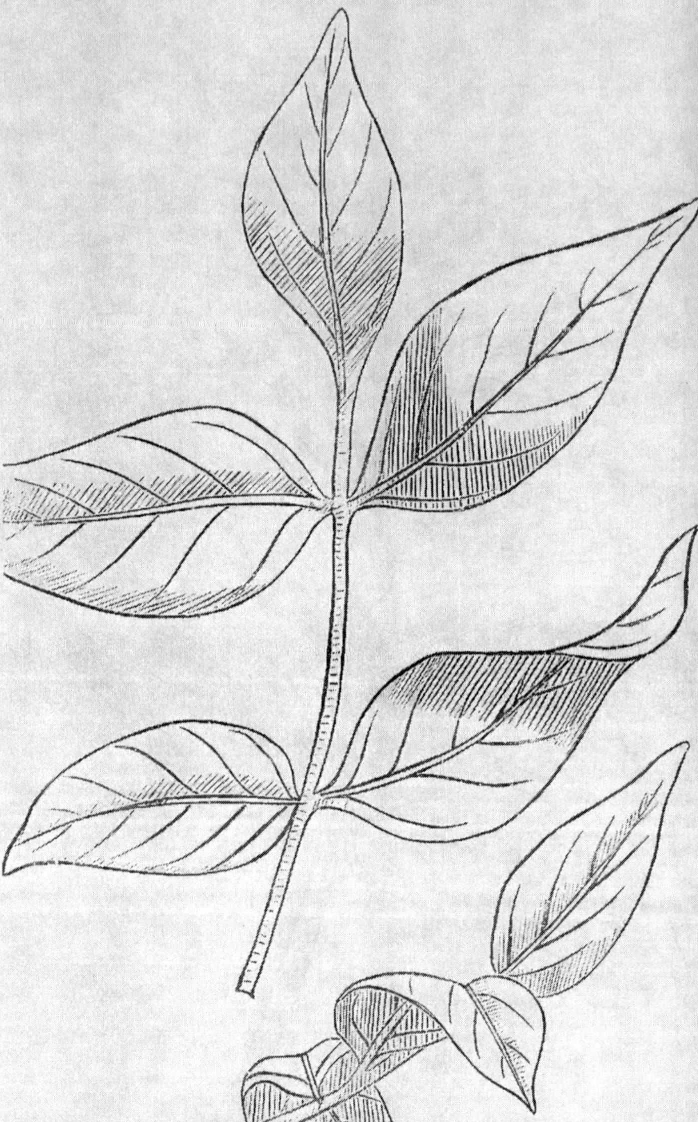

Ordina wodier.

PLATE XLVIII.

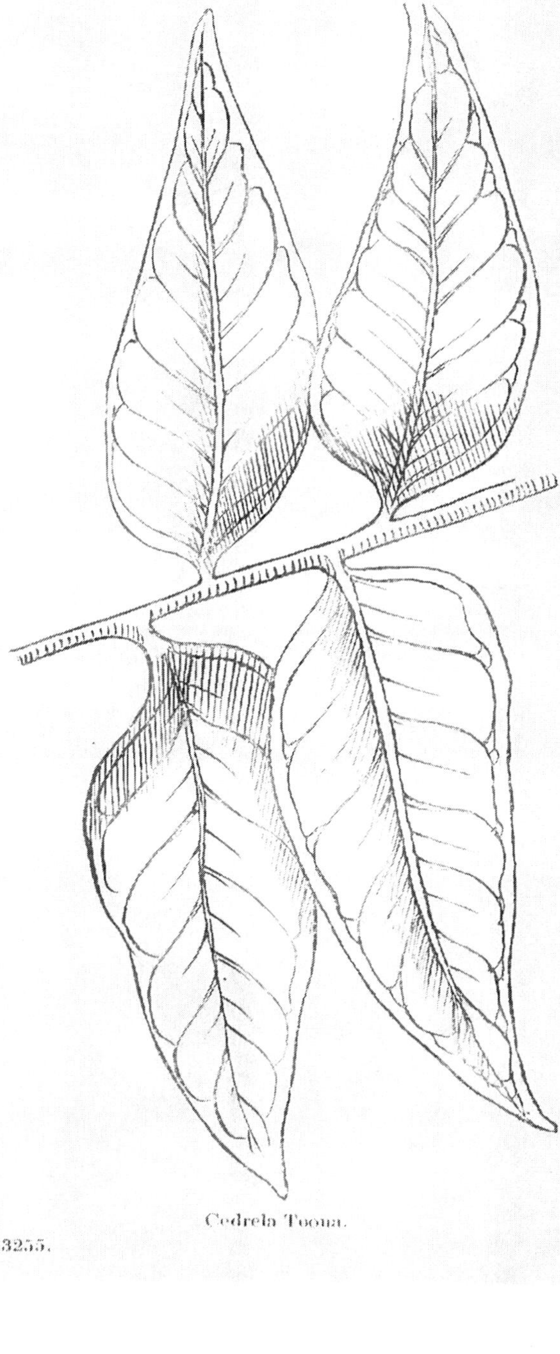

Cedrela Toona.

PLATE XLIX.

FIG. 1.

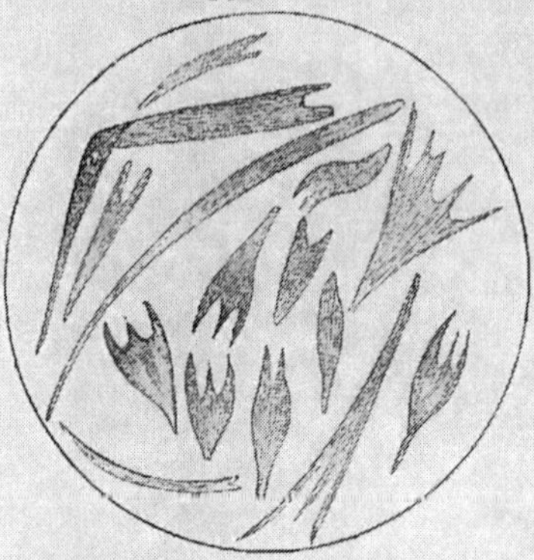

Bombyx mori (Male).

FIG. 2.

Antheræa mylitta (Male).

FIG. 3.

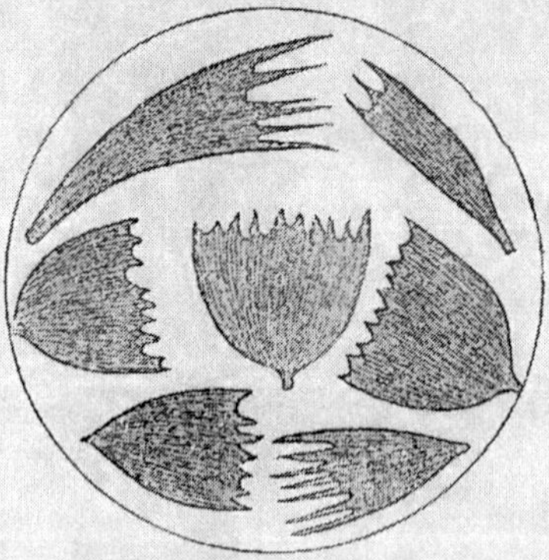

Antheræa mylitta (Female).

FIG. 4.

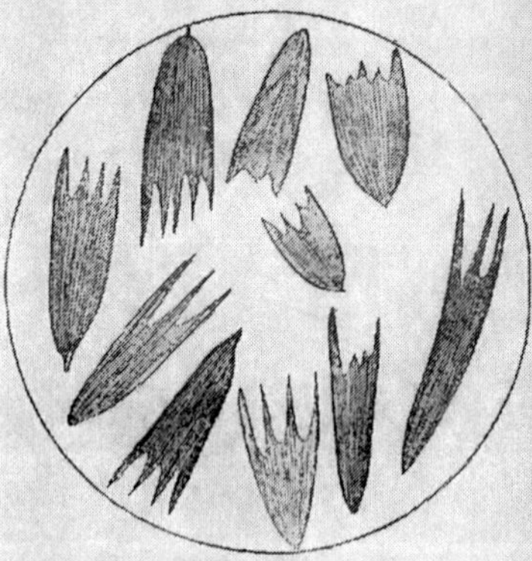

Attacus ricini (Male).

FIG. 5.

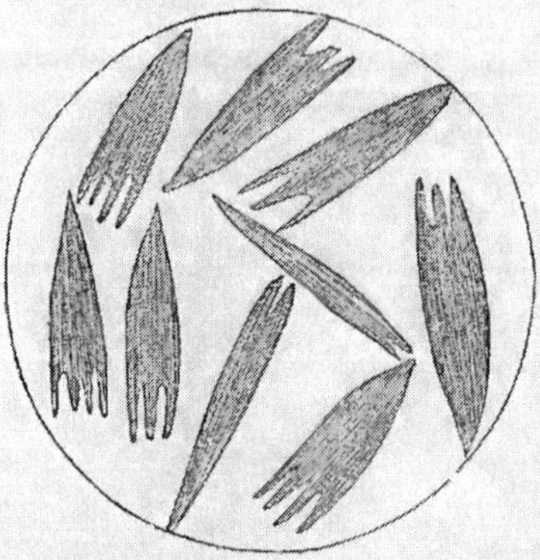

Attacus cynthia (Male).

FIG. 6.

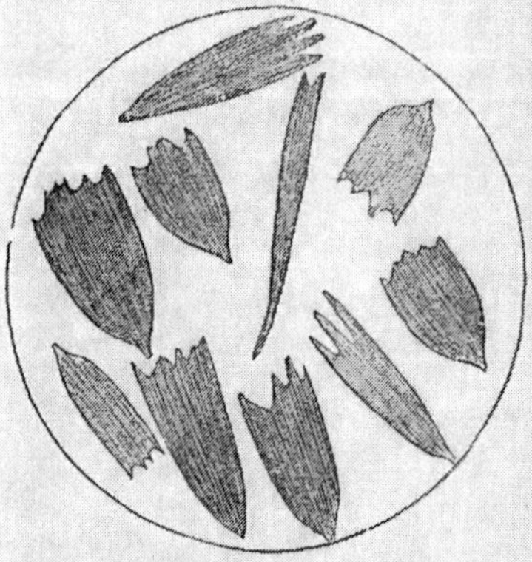

Attacus Atlas (Male).

Scales from Wings magnified 140 diameters.

PLATE I.

FIG. 1.

Attacus Atlas (Female).

FIG. 2.

Antheræa pernyi (Male).

FIG. 3.

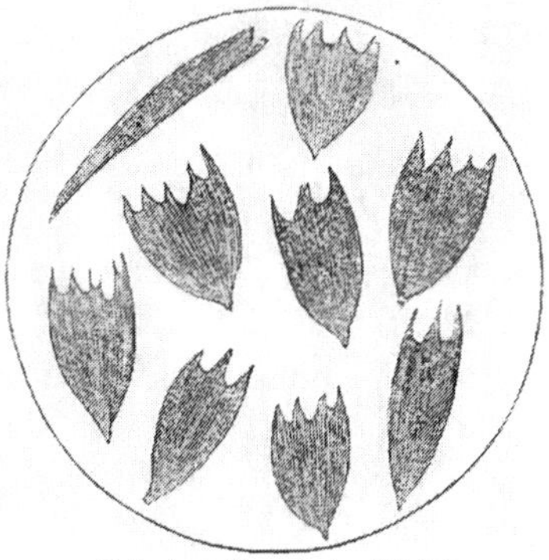

Cricula trifenestrata (Male).

FIG. 4.

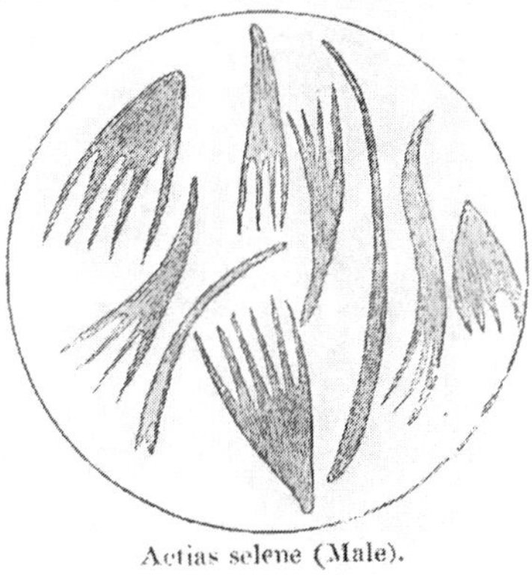

Actias selene (Male).

FIG. 5.

Antheræa yama-mai (Male).

FIG. 6.

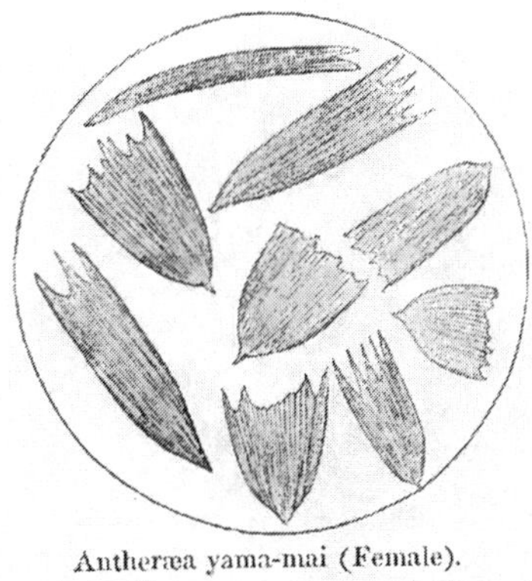

Antheræa yama-mai (Female).

Scales from Wings magnified 140 diameters.

PLATE LI.

Fig. 1.

Saturnia carpini (Male).

Fig. 2.

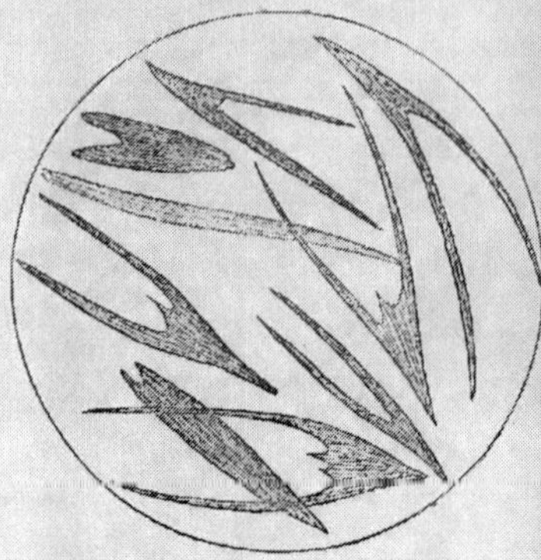

Saturnia carpini (Female).

Fig. 3.

Antheræa Roylei (Male).

Fig. 4.

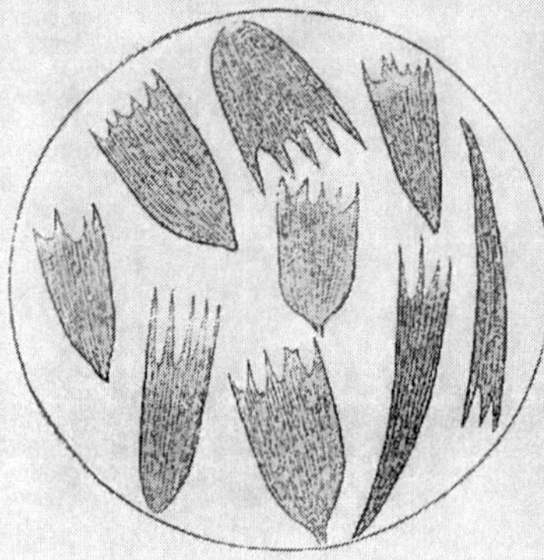

Antheræa Helferi (Male).

Fig. 5.

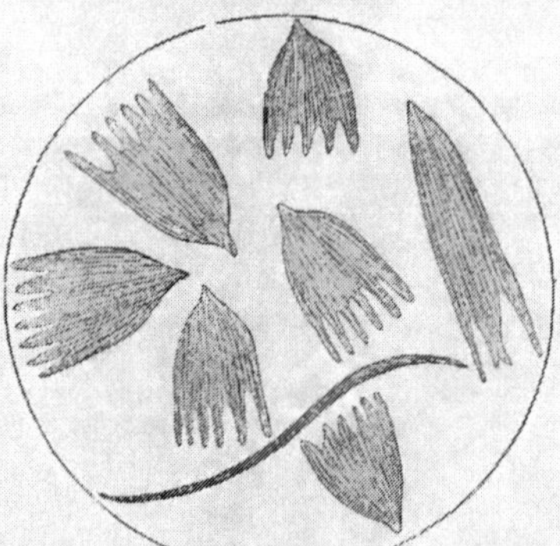

Loepa katinka (Male).

Fig. 6.

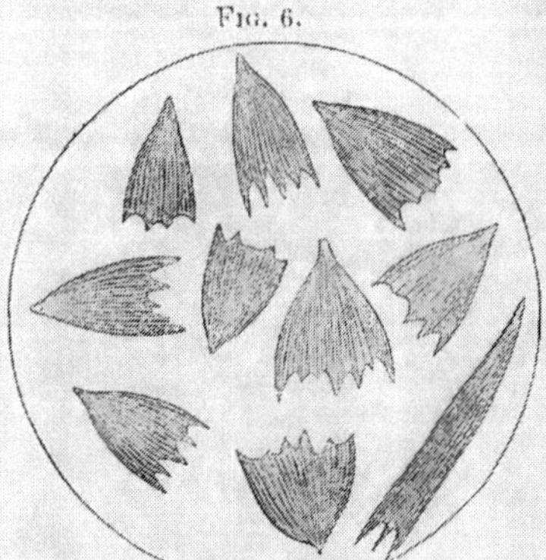

Loepa miranda (Male).

Scales from Wings magnified 140 diameters.

PLATE LII.

FIG. 1.

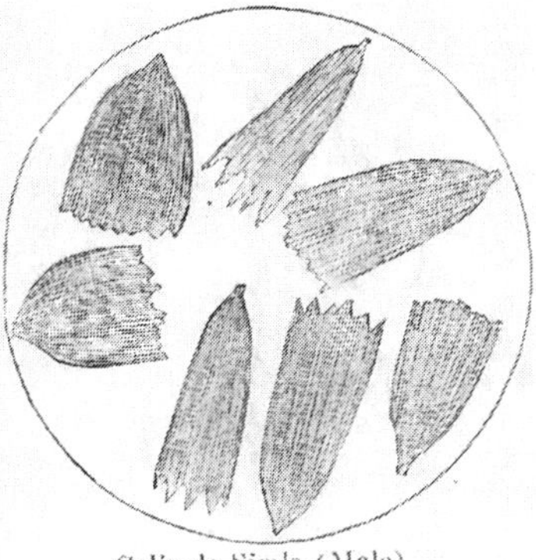

Caligula Simla (Male).

FIG. 2.

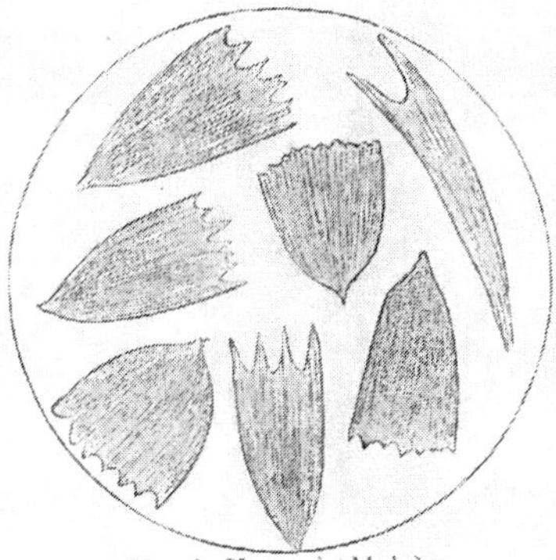

Neoris Huttoni (Male).

FIG. 3.

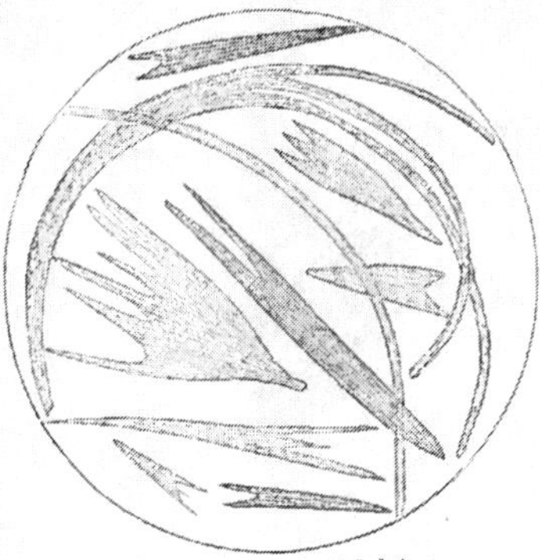

Bombyx mori (Male).

FIG. 4.

Antheræa mylitta (Male).

Taken from different parts of Wing.

FIG. 5.

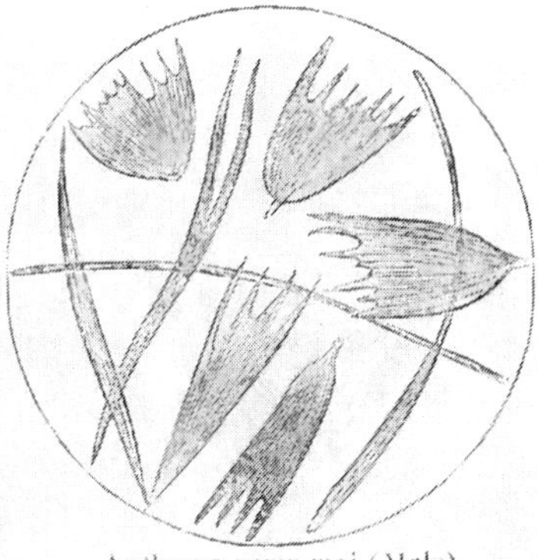

Antheræa yama-mai (Male).

FIG. 6.

Actias selene (Male).

Taken from different parts of Wing.

Scales from Wings magnified 140 diameters.

PLATE LIII.

FIG. 1.

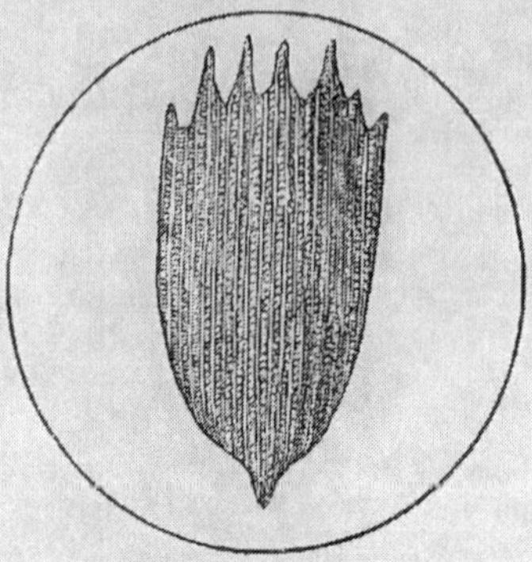

Attacus Atlas (Male).

FIG. 2.

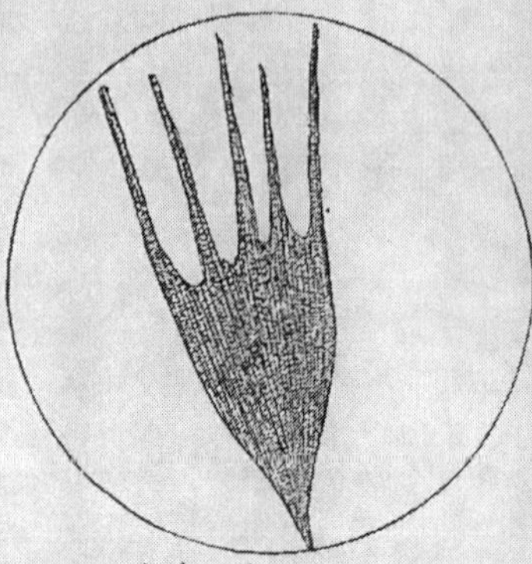

Actias selene (Male).

FIG. 3.

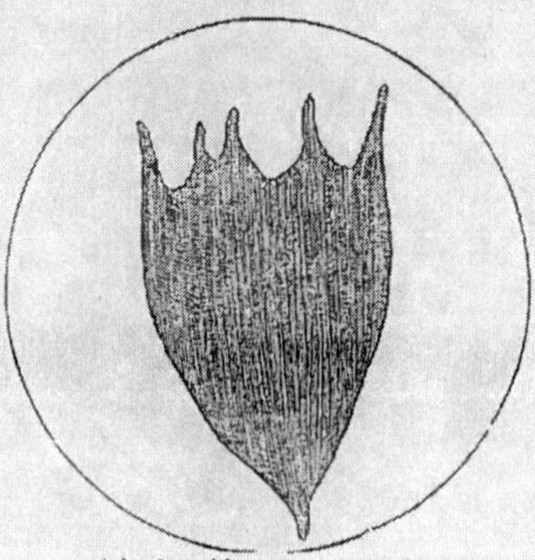

Crieula trifenestrata (Male).

FIG. 4.

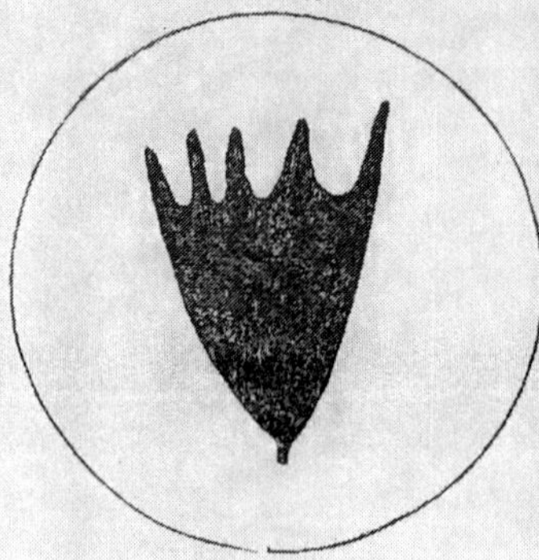

Saturnia carpini (Male).

FIG. 5.

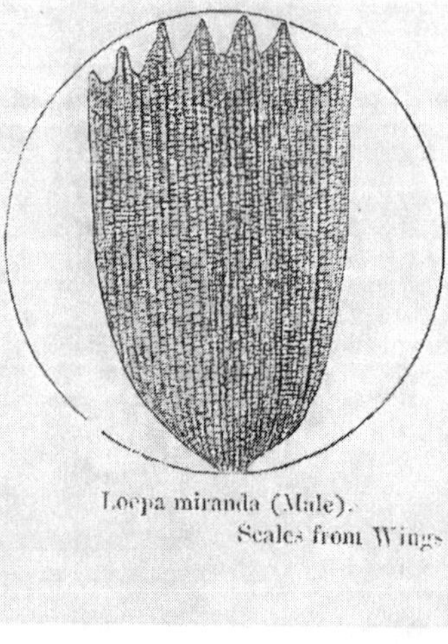

Loepa miranda (Male).

FIG. 6.

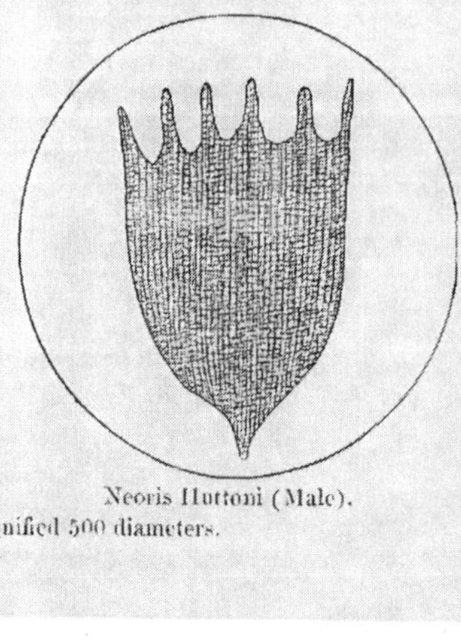

Neoris Huttoni (Male).

Scales from Wings magnified 500 diameters.

PLATE LIV.

FIG. 1.

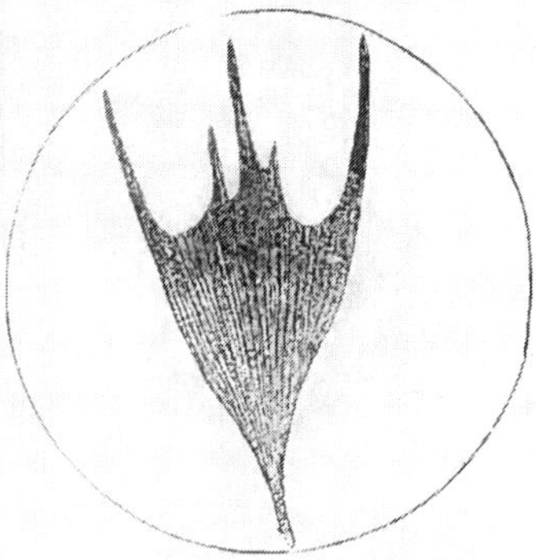

Bombyx mori (Male).

FIG. 2.

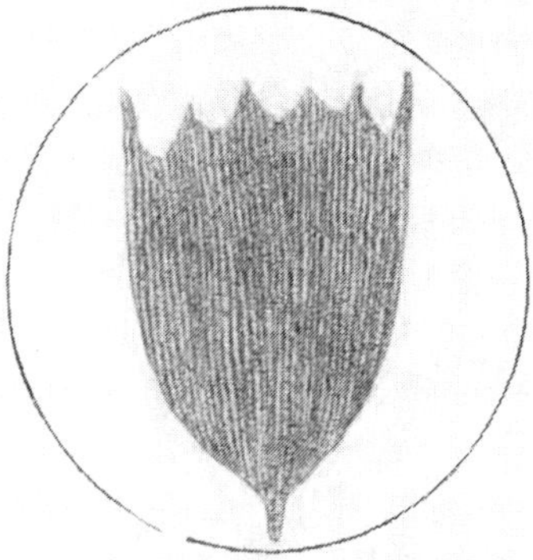

Antheræa mylitta (Male).

FIG. 3.

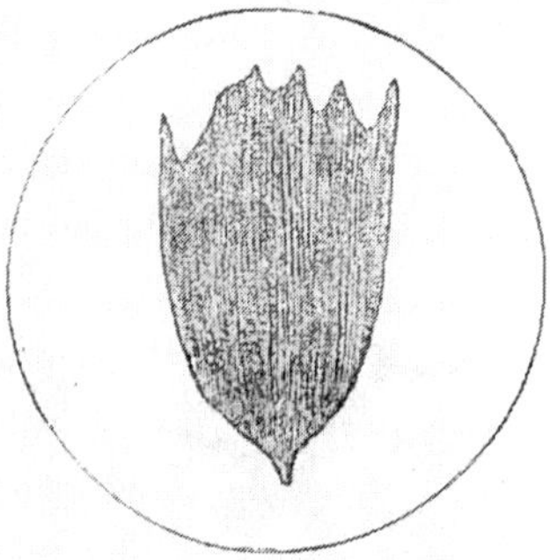

Antheræa pernyi (Male).

FIG. 4.

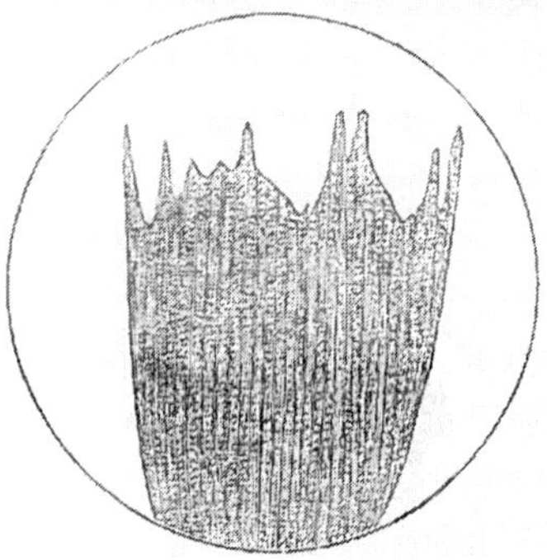

Antheræa Roylei (Male).

FIG. 5.

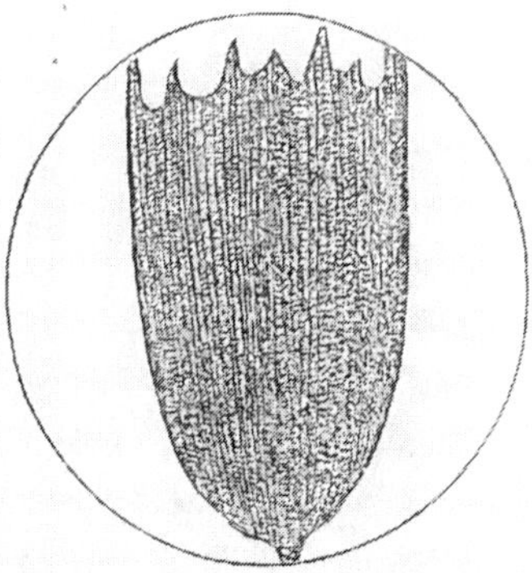

Antheræa yama-mai.

FIG. 6.

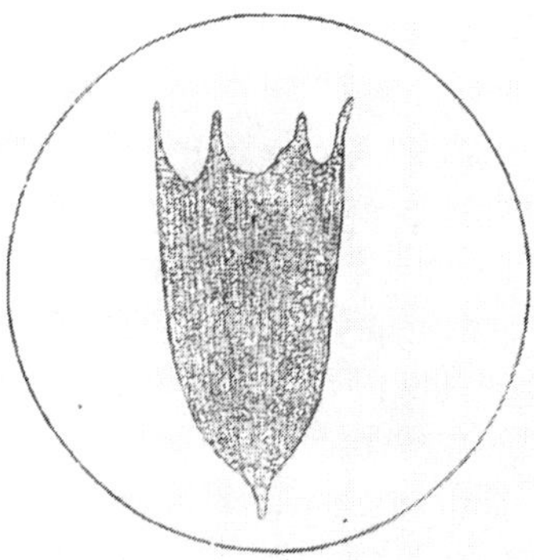

Attacus ricini (Male).

Scales from Wings magnified 500 diameters.

PLATE LV.

Tusser on Tusser embroidery.

PLATE LVI.

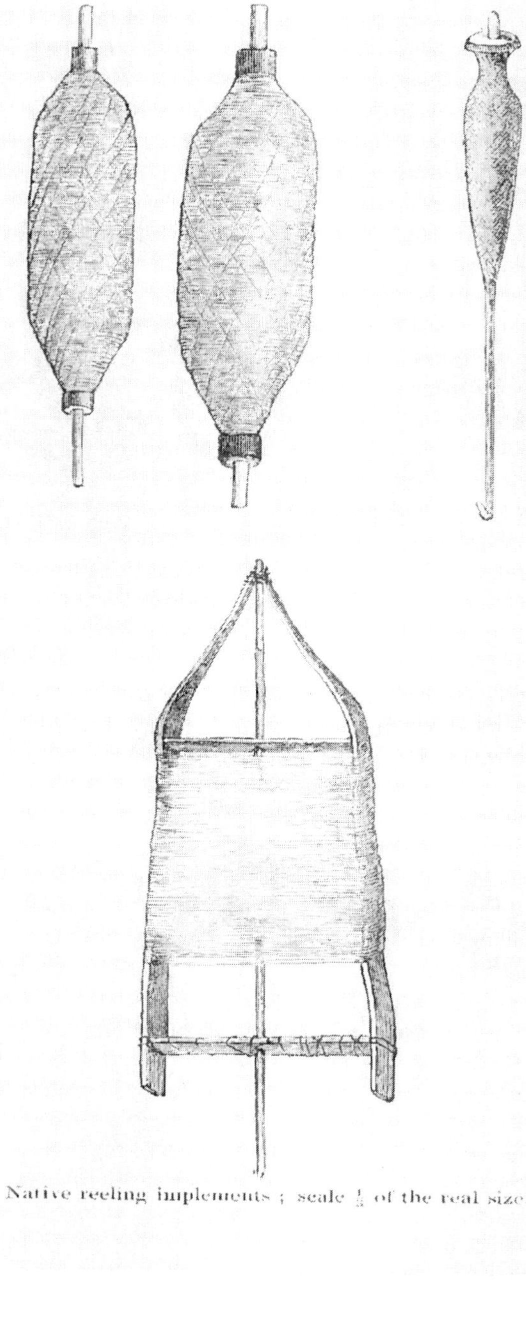

Native reeling implements ; scale ⅓ of the real size.

PLATE LVII.

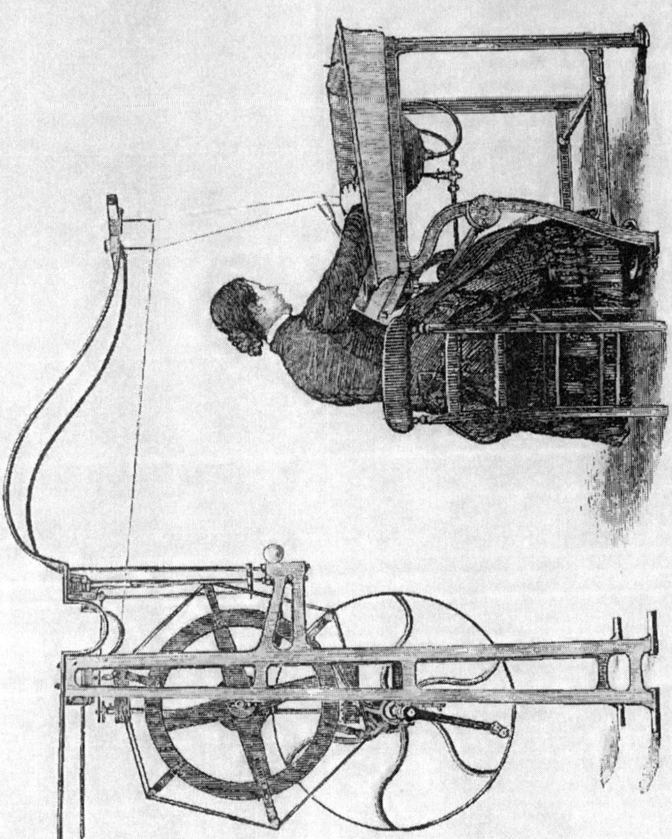

Cocoon-reeling machine, side view.

PLATE LVIII.

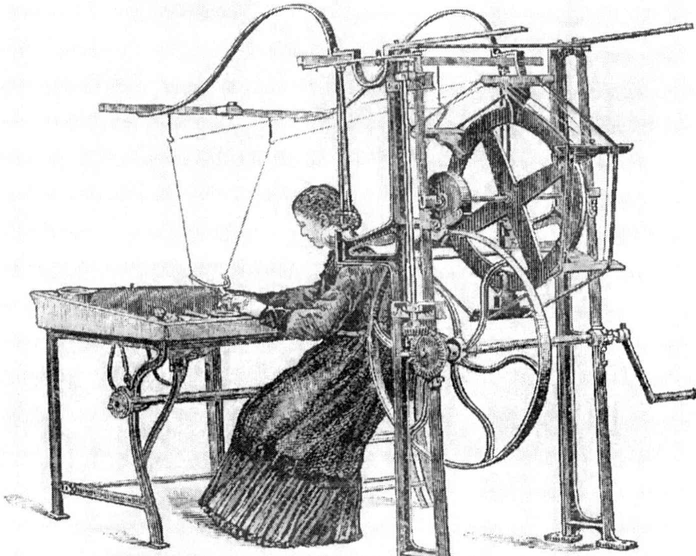

Cocoon-reeling machine, diagonal view.

PLATE LIX.

Brass vessels belonging to tray; scale ½ of the real size.

PLATE LX.

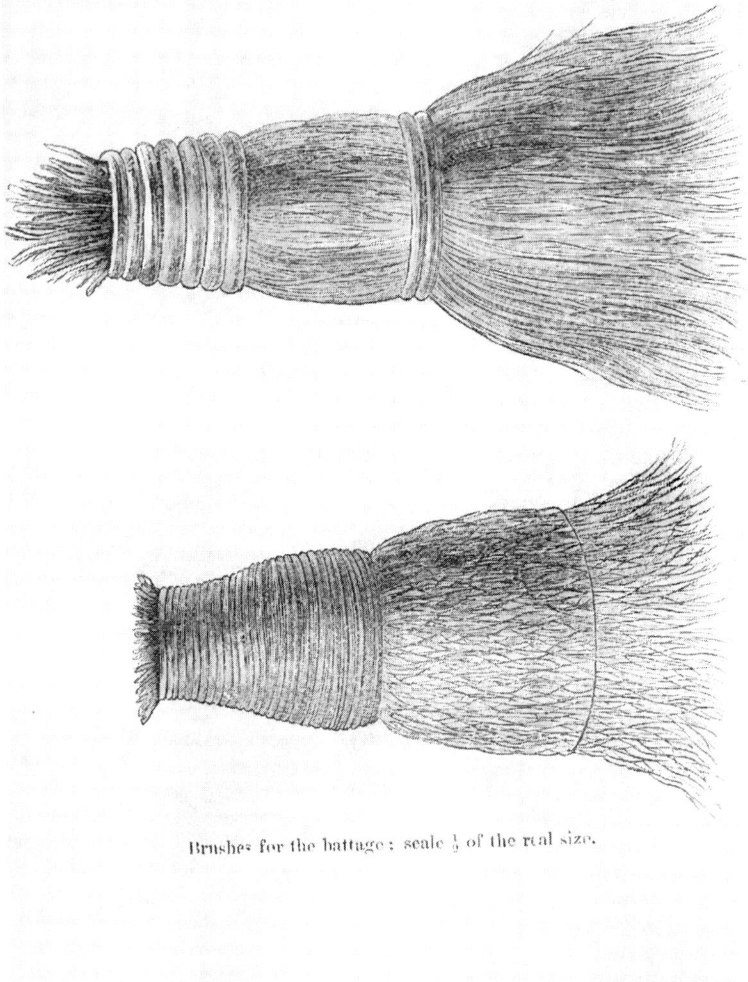

Brushes for the battage; scale ½ of the real size.

PLATE LXI.

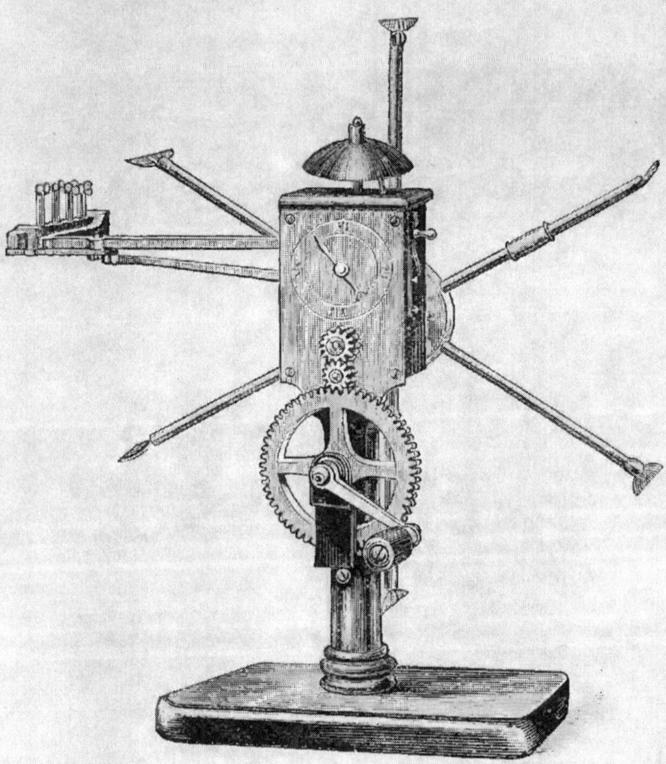

Measuring reel ; scale $\frac{1}{5}$ of the real size.

PLATE LXII.

FIG. 1.

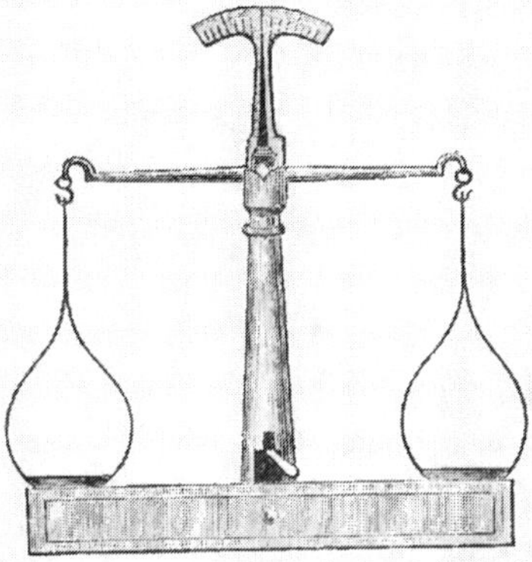

Fine balance for deniering; scale $\frac{1}{3}$ of real size.

FIG. 2.

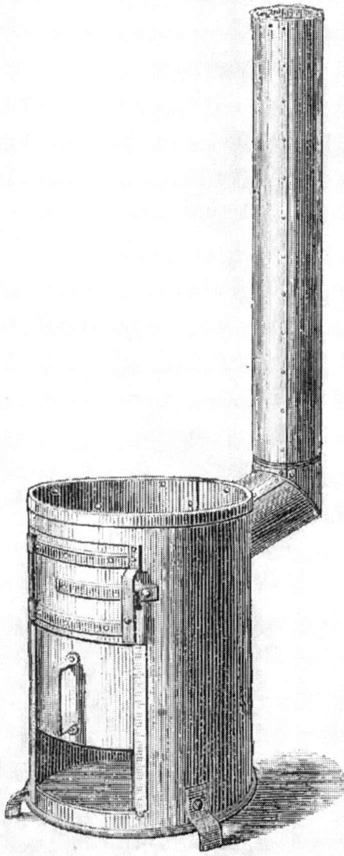

Stove for heating basin; scale 1 inch to the foot.

PLATE LXIII.

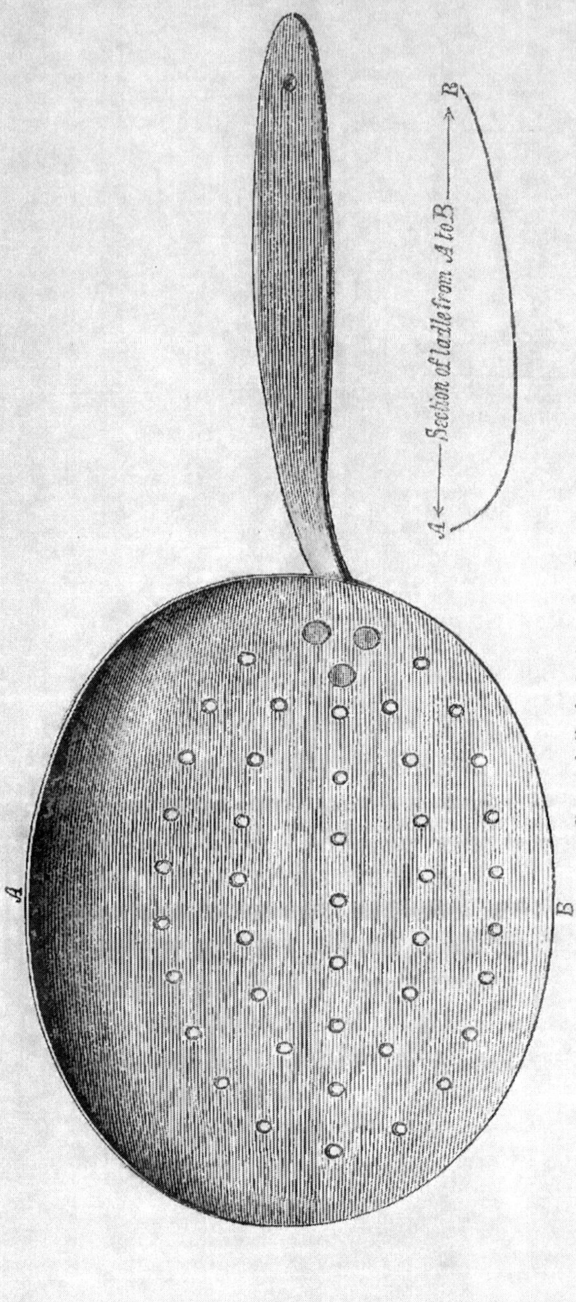

Cocoon ladle for basin ; scale $\frac{1}{3}$ of the real size.

PLATE LXIV.

Fig. 1.

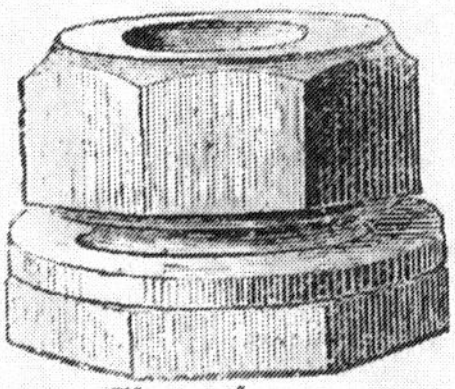

Champignon ;
scale ½ natural size.

Fig. 2.

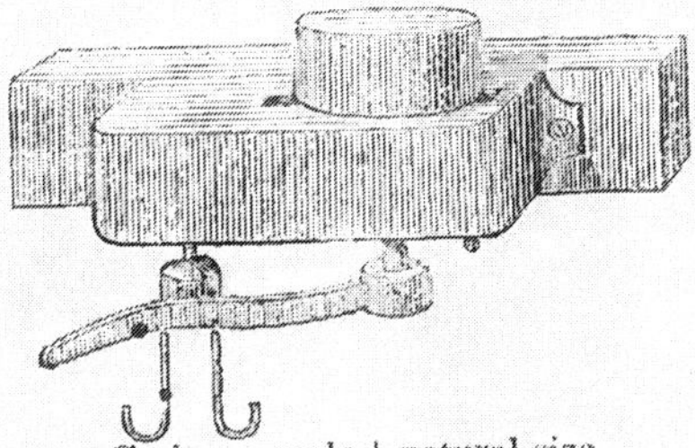

Croiseur, scale ½ natural size.

Fig. 3.

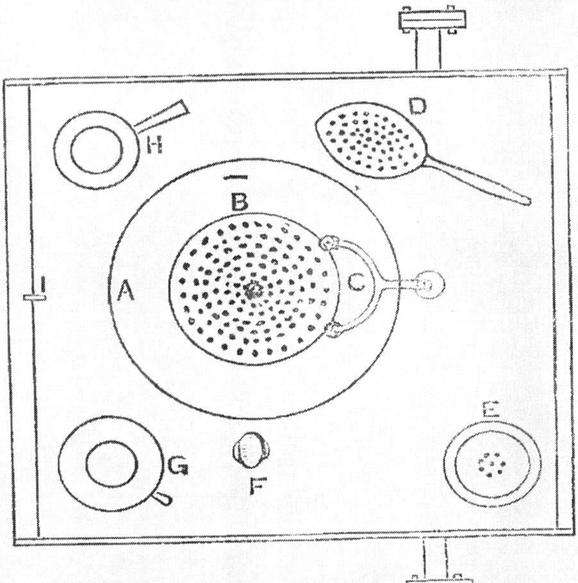

Tray and utensils ; mechanical drawing, scale 1 inch to the foot.

PLATE LXV.

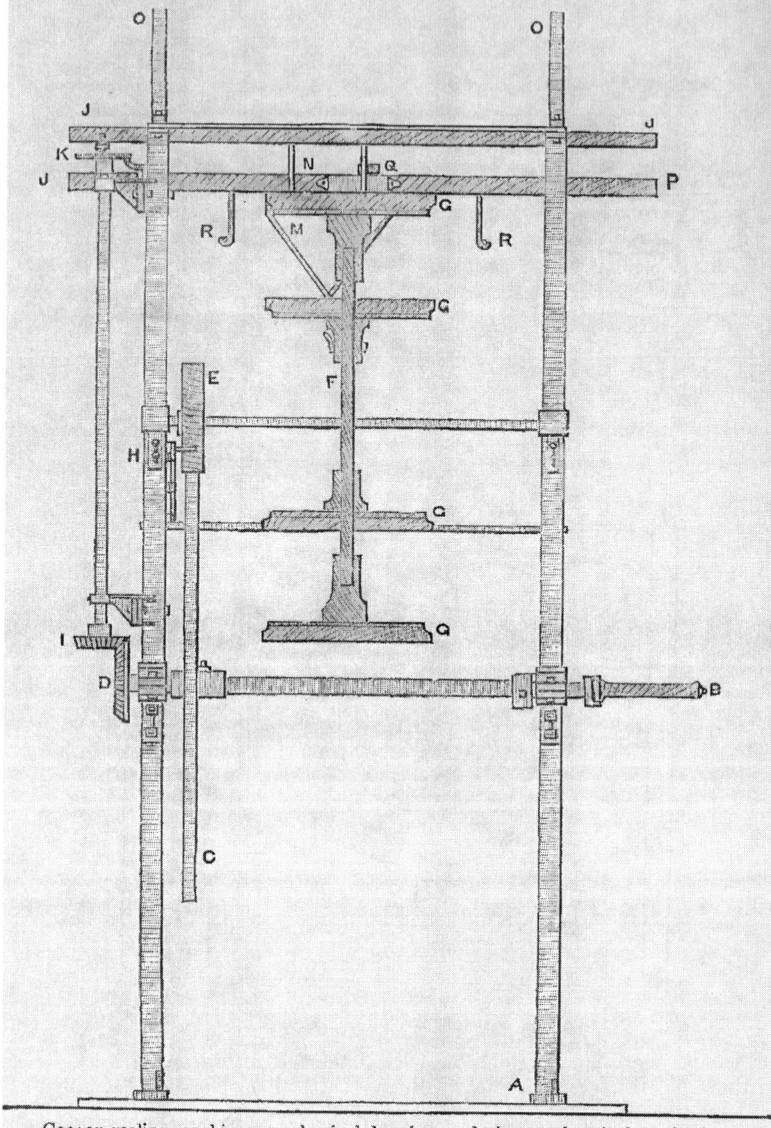

Cocoon-reeling machine; mechanical drawing, end view, scale 1 inch to the foot.

PLATE LXVI.

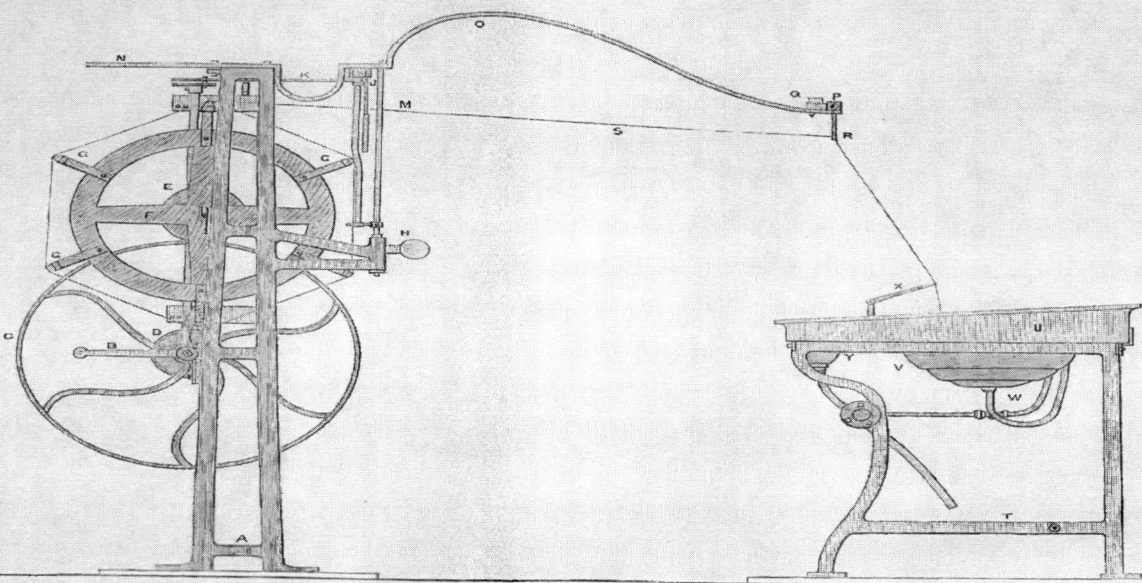

Cocoon-reeling machine ; mechanical drawing, side view, scale 1 inch to the foot.

Q 3255.